# cycling in the peak district
## off-road trails & quiet lanes    written by tom fenton & jon barton

VERTEBRATE **PUBLISHING**

Design and production by Vertebrate Publishing, Sheffield.
www.**v-publishing**.co.uk

# cycling in the peak district

off-road trails & quiet Lanes    written by tom fenton & jon barton

ISBN: 978-1-906148-00-3

Cover photo by John Houlihan
Photography by John Houlihan

Design & production by Paul Mellor
Edited by Tom Fenton
Vertebrate Publishing
www.**v-publishing**.co.uk

VERTEBRATE PUBLISHING

**MIX**
Paper from
responsible sources
FSC® C016973
FSC
www.fsc.org

# contents

# introduction

We've been cycling in the Peak District for over a decade and a half, and we don't intend to stop any time soon. It's a great place to ride a bike.

The riding here stretches from rides on tarmac and quiet cycleways to twisting trails through the woods and big rocky bridleways tumbling down off the moors. There are bike-friendly cafés, tiny villages whose shops seem to stock just the right amount of cake to revive tired riders and some great pubs where you can follow a big day out with an equally large meal.

You can go out for a ride through the dramatic Dark Peak and meet dozens of like-minded people, or you can head to the White Peak and wind your way through its Limestone Dales without seeing a single soul. Get away from it all or be buoyed along by fellow enthusiasts – which would you prefer?

Then there's the weather. No matter what time of year it is, the Peak always looks good. In the summer, the fields and woodland of the White Peak come alive, whereas the Dark Peak is arguably at its best on a clear winter's day, when the ground is frozen solid. Come in spring or autumn and see either lambs or a landscape full of colour.

We could go on all day. We've written this book because we want you to enjoy riding in the Peak as much as we do. See you out there.

**Tom Fenton** & **Jon Barton**

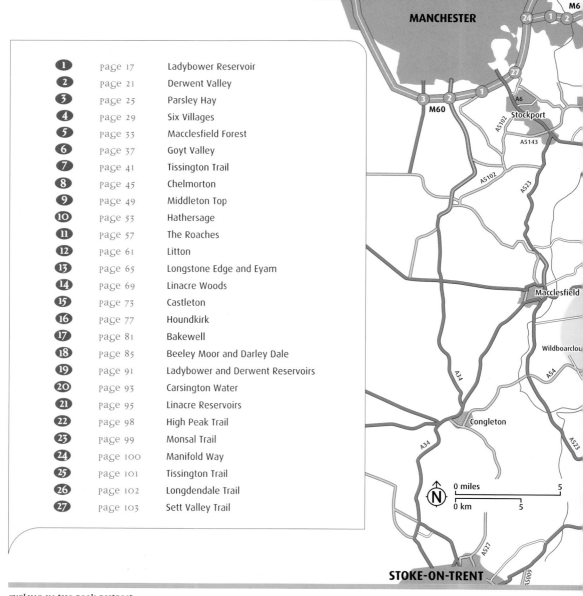

MANCHESTER
M6
24 1 2
27
M60
Stockport
A6
A5102
A5143
A5102
A523
Macclesfield
Wildboarclou
A34
A54
Congleton
A34
A523
0 miles 5
N
0 km 5
STOKE-ON-TRENT
A527
A5009

# a note on the rides

This book is aimed at novice and intermediate riders. If you've got young children with you, turn straight to our family section on page 91. Otherwise, the routes are ordered by difficulty, so start at the front and work your way through the book. The easier routes should be well within the capabilities or every rider, while still being enjoyable enough to keep more advanced cyclists entertained. Towards the back of the book, the routes are longer and venture off-road more often. These routes will challenge better riders – and will be well within the capabilities of the novice who has worked his or her way through the book.

It is worth noting that this is the Peak District – it's (very) hilly, and the off-road sections can be rocky, so don't expect any of the rides to be as gentle as they might be in other areas of the country. So, treat them as a challenge and enjoy the unique landscape created by these rocks and hills – you'll have fun and quickly become a fitter and more proficient rider.

Each route is a mixture of quiet, mainly traffic-free lanes and bridleways. As is the way with national parks and sunny periods, the off-road sections will be more rideable in dry weather, but the road riding will be busier.

Most rides are circular, starting and finishing at an appropriate spot with convenient parking. Some have pubs or cafés at various points along the way, others picnic spots.

# maps, descriptions, distances

While every effort has been made to ensure accuracy within the maps and descriptions in this guide, things change and we are unable to guarantee that every detail is correct. Treat stated distances as guidelines. We strongly recommend that you carry a detailed map of the area with you when riding and do not rely solely on this guide. A 'proper' map will provide more information and help you find your way if you get lost and ride off the maps included here.

# your bike

Any bike will get you round the easier routes in this book, provided it works. It you're going to venture off-road, we'd recommend a mountain bike, as the increased toughness and comfort will pay dividends. To an extent, the more you pay, the more fun you'll have, if only because very cheap bikes are heavy and unreliable.

Check that everything works – you won't be going anywhere fast if your gears seize, but you'll probably be a little quicker than planned if your brakes fail... Pump the tyres up, check they aren't about to wear through and ensure that everything that should be tight is tight. If you're not sure you can do this yourself, visit your local bike shop.

# CLothing

You need to get your clothing right if you want to stay comfortable on a bike, especially in bad weather.

Ideally, you should choose clothing made from 'technical' synthetic or wool fabrics which 'wick' or draw the sweat away from your body and then dry quickly, preventing you from getting cold and damp. Stay away from cotton, as it absorbs moisture and then holds onto it, becoming heavy, uncomfortable and cold. If it's chilly, wear a layer of thin fleece on top to keep you warm, and then a wind/waterproof on top of this, to keep out the elements.

As cycling is an active sport, it's worth setting off just a little on the cool side as you'll soon warm up on the first hill. Don't leave the warm clothes behind though, as the weather could turn and they'll keep you warm on lunch stops.

## gLoves

Cycling gloves help prevent blisters and numb hands and keep your fingers warm. They also provide a surprising amount of protection if you fall off.

## otHer essentiaLs

Take any necessary spare parts for your bike, tools and a pump. We'd suggest taking a spare inner tube, as it's far quicker to swop tubes than to stop and repair a puncture. Be aware that children's bikes may have smaller wheels than yours and may need different tubes! Also consider spare clothes, a first aid kit and make sure you have enough food and water.

You'll need something to carry this little lot in. We'd suggest a rucksack as many are now compatible with water 'bladders' which allow you to drink on the move via a tube and mouthpiece. Panniers, on the other hand, keep the weight off you and on your bike, although they can bounce around and make the bike unwieldy on rough ground. Whatever you choose, make sure it's big enough to carry everything, including any excess clothing you may be wearing.

# route map key

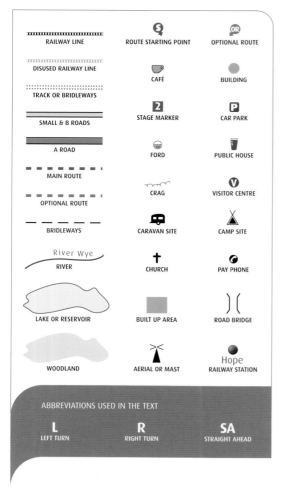

| | | |
|---|---|---|
| RAILWAY LINE | ROUTE STARTING POINT | OPTIONAL ROUTE |
| DISUSED RAILWAY LINE | CAFÉ | BUILDING |
| TRACK OR BRIDLEWAYS | STAGE MARKER | CAR PARK |
| SMALL & B ROADS | FORD | PUBLIC HOUSE |
| A ROAD | CRAG | VISITOR CENTRE |
| MAIN ROUTE | CARAVAN SITE | CAMP SITE |
| OPTIONAL ROUTE | CHURCH | PAY PHONE |
| BRIDLEWAYS | BUILT UP AREA | ROAD BRIDGE |
| River Wye RIVER | | |
| LAKE OR RESERVOIR | | |
| WOODLAND | AERIAL OR MAST | Hope RAILWAY STATION |

**ABBREVIATIONS USED IN THE TEXT**

| L | R | SA |
|---|---|---|
| LEFT TURN | RIGHT TURN | STRAIGHT AHEAD |

# rights of way

Countryside access in the UK hasn't been particularly kind to cyclists, although things are improving. We have 'right of way' on bridleways (blue arrows on signs) and byways (red arrows). However, having 'right of way' doesn't actually mean having **the** right of way, just that we're allowed to ride there – so give way to walkers and horse riders. We're also allowed to ride on green lanes and some unclassified roads, although the only way to determine which are legal and which aren't is to check with the local countryside authority.

Everything else – footpaths, open countryside and so forth is, sadly, out of bounds.

# rules of the (off) road

- Always ride on legal trails.
- Ride considerately – give way to horses and pedestrians.
- Don't spook animals.
- Ride in control – you don't know who's around the next corner.
- Leave gates as you find them – if you're unsure, shut them.
- Keep the noise down and don't swear loudly when you fall off in front of walkers.
- Leave no trace – take home everything you took out.
- Keep water sources clean – don't take toilet stops near streams.
- Enjoy the countryside and respect its life and work.

# general safety (a.k.a. 'common sense')

Cycling can be dangerous. Too much exuberance on a descent in the middle of nowhere could leave you in more than a spot of bother. Consider your limitations and relative fragility before launching at something.

Carry food and water, spares, a tube and pump. Consider a first-aid kit. Even if it's warm, the weather could turn, so take a wind/waterproof. Think about what could happen on an enforced stop. Pack lights if you could finish in the dark, as over-ambitious family trips often do.

The ability to map-read, navigate and understand weather warnings is essential. Don't go out in bad weather unless you're confident and capable of doing so.

While these routes keep to quiet lanes as much as is possible, roads in this region can be very busy. Plan accordingly, obey the Highway Code and assume the majority of drivers are idiots...

If riding alone, think about the potential seriousness of an accident – you could be without help for a long time. Tell someone where you're going and when you'll be back. Take a phone if you have one, but don't rely on getting a signal. (And don't call out mountain rescue because you've grazed your knee.)

Riding in a group is safer (ambitious overtaking manoeuvres excepted) and often more fun, but don't leave slower riders behind and give them a breather when they've caught up.

When choosing your route, check the weather, the amount of daylight/time available and the ability/ experience of each rider. Allow more time than you think necessary to allow for problems.

As the area is popular, ride in control and give way to others. Bells might be annoying, but they work. If you can't bring yourself to bolt one on, a polite 'excuse me' should be fine.

On hot, sunny days, make sure that you slap some Factor 30+ and **ALWAYS WEAR YOUR HELMET!**

## Mountain Rescue
In the event of an accident requiring mountain rescue assistance:
Dial 999 and ask for POLICE – MOUNTAIN RESCUE.

# the routes

Welcome to the Peak. The following routes are spread right across the National Park, allowing you to explore every part of this fantastic area of countryside. Gradually increasing in difficulty through the book, these rides will take you through limestone dales, along old railway lines – reminders of the Peak's industrial era – and up towards the gritstone moors. Enjoy!

# Ladybower Reservoir

Route 1 // 12km

**Sitting right in the centre of the Dark Peak, this relatively quiet 'there and back' family ride runs along the southern bank of Ladybower Reservoir. Taking good, wide tracks, the route undulates along the shore of the reservoir with some lovely views out over the water.**

This is not a long ride and could be completed by fast riders in under an hour, making it ideal for families, novices or those wanting to combine a short ride in the country with a pub lunch. There are two pubs very close to the start – and therefore end – of the ride, and some nice picnic spots along the way. Beginning on tarmac, the trail soon turns to a well-surfaced dirt and stone track, with a few hills and swooping descents to keep things interesting.

For more adventurous riders, an optional return route climbs steeply uphill away from the reservoir (it's rideable, it just takes a bit of oomph) to take some narrow singletrack trails through the wood as it winds its way back down towards the start of the ride. This option will add a little time and a lot of effort to the route, but no real distance. Expect mud, some small rocks and narrow trails!

The ride starts from Heatherdene car park, which is on your right as you approach the large bridge across Ladybower Reservoir on the A6013.

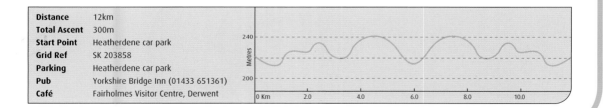

| Distance | 12km |
|---|---|
| Total Ascent | 300m |
| Start Point | Heatherdene car park |
| Grid Ref | SK 203858 |
| Parking | Heatherdene car park |
| Pub | Yorkshire Bridge Inn (01433 651361) |
| Café | Fairholmes Visitor Centre, Derwent |

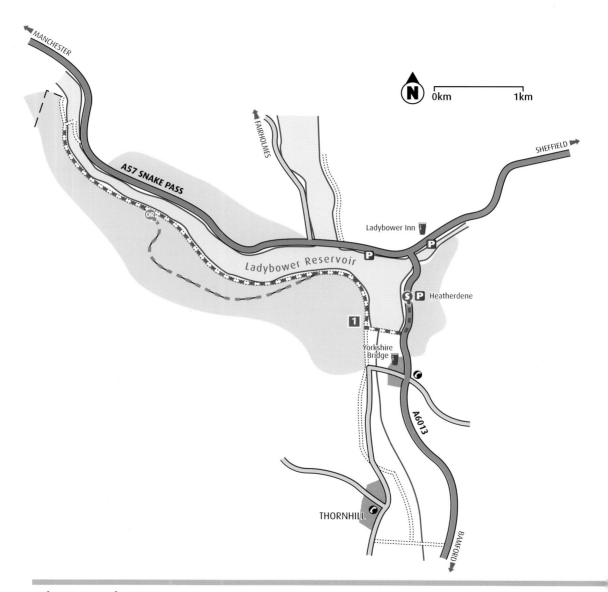

MANCHESTER

N
0km     1km

SHEFFIELD

FAIRHOLMES

A57 SNAKE PASS

OR

Ladybower Inn

P

P

Ladybower Reservoir

S P Heatherdene

1

Yorkshire Bridge

A6013

BAMFORD

THORNHILL

Leave the car park and cross the road to the cycle path. Turn **L** and ride to the steps and gates that allow access to the dam. The signs here ask cyclists to dismount and push across the dam as the path along the top is not a cycleway or bridleway. Turn **R** once through the gate on the far side.

**1** Follow the track, initially on tarmac and then on a good stone surface along the side of Ladybower in an increasingly picturesque setting. There are several spots along the way that would make great picnic stops.

The track undulates throughout its length and eventually descends to a fork at a gate. It's here that this short ride ends, so you'll need to make a u-turn and retrace your tyre tracks to your car.

**Optional return route:** If you're feeling fit and adventurous and you are prepared to get muddy, there's a good alternative return route. It involves some very steep climbing, some tricky and slippery descending and can get very muddy, although it isn't long.

Climb from the gate to the crest of the hill to where a wide area of felled woodland gives way to trees. Turn **R** up a very steep and straight permissive bridleway (a pictorial sign depicts a walker, a bicycle and a horseshoe).

Climb very steeply through the woods to an open area. Continue **SA** over the crossroads into the woods ahead and follow the track around to the left as it turns to singletrack and becomes vague.

After a short and steep descent, ignore the turning to the left and continue **SA** along singletrack, eventually descending to rejoin the main track along the side of Ladybower. Turn **R** and retrace you steps to your car.

## LocaL knowLeDGe

Towards the start of this ride, you will cross Ladybower Dam. Built in 1943, its construction flooded the upper Derwent Valley, submerging two villages in the process, and creating Ladybower Reservoir, which provides water for Sheffield, Nottingham, Derby and Leicester. At the time, it was the largest reservoir in the country, taking two years to fill with water.

## famiLy RIDING

This is an easy ride on a relatively good surface. Although the surface is slightly looser and hillier than the cycleways in the south Peak, it is very rideable. The choice of two pubs near the start/finish of the ride and the picnic spots – of the picnic-blanket variety, rather than the table and bench type – mean that this track would make a nice, gentle outing for a family.

## makING a Day of it

The Derwent Valley ride is within cycling distance of this route and the two could be combined to make a long, though technically easy day out.

Ladybower reservoir near fairholmes

# Derwent Valley

## Route 2 // 16km (8km extension)

**A superb and popular ride around the most famous reservoirs in the Dark Peak. Starting at Fairholmes** (café, bike hire and ducks to feed)**, the ride heads north, on tarmac, up the western sides of Derwent and Howden reservoirs. It's all very picturesque, pretty and peaceful, soon becoming a little wilder as the tarmac ends. From here, wide, fairly smooth dirt tracks are followed around the top of Howden Reservoir and similar tracks undulate along the eastern side of the valley until Derwent Dam allows a return to Fairholmes by road. There are some great views out over the reservoirs, some impressive dams to see and a dollop of history – it was here that the RAF practiced with their 'bouncing bombs' in preparation for the famous Dambuster raids in Germany during WWII.**

Much of the ride is on tarmac with little traffic, and the remainder is on easy dirt tracks that have warning signs before any descents. It's not flat, though, with a small amount climbing to be tackled.

If you're feeling energetic, you can continue down the eastern side of Derwent Valley, past Ladybower Reservoir to the Snake Pass and then back up the road to Fairholmes.

The route starts at Fairholmes. To reach it, find your way to Ladybower and turn right immediately after crossing the long bridge over the reservoirs on the A57, heading towards Manchester.

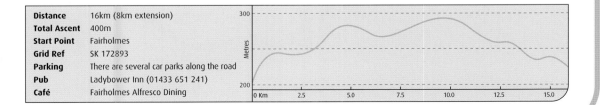

| | |
|---|---|
| **Distance** | 16km (8km extension) |
| **Total Ascent** | 400m |
| **Start Point** | Fairholmes |
| **Grid Ref** | SK 172893 |
| **Parking** | There are several car parks along the road |
| **Pub** | Ladybower Inn (01433 651 241) |
| **Café** | Fairholmes Alfresco Dining |

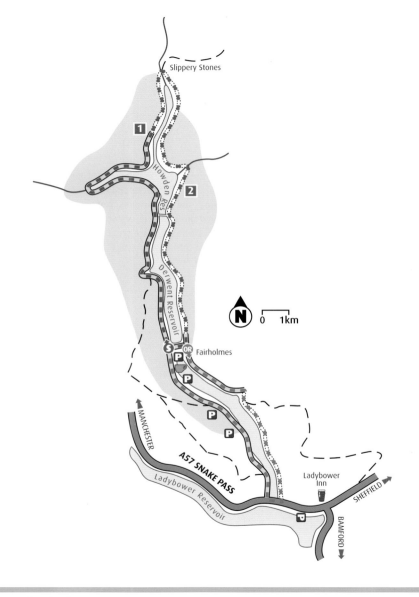

Slippery Stones

1

2

Howden Res

Derwent Reservoir

N
0    1km

S OR P Fairholmes
P

P

P

MANCHESTER

A57 SNAKE PASS

Ladybower Reservoir

Ladybower Inn

SHEFFIELD

BAMFORD

Turn **R** out of Fairholmes and head up the Derwent Valley on the road, going **SA** over the roundabout and through the gate.

**1** Follow tarmac, for some distance, to a roundabout/turning area and go **SA** through the gate onto a gravel track.

This track ends at two gates. Go through the RH gate, marked Cyclists Please Walk and descend to a bridge. Cross the bridge, head **L** and then turn back **R** on yourself, following signs marked Cyclists.

**2** Follow the track through gates until you join tarmac. Take the next **R** (sharply back on yourself), signed Fairholmes Cycle Hire and follow the road round past the base of the dam to Fairholmes.

**Optional route:** Continue **SA** on tarmac, passing through gates and onto more dirt tracks until you reach the Snake Pass. Turn **R** on the cycle path across the bridge spanning the gap between the two halves of Ladybower Reservoir, paying attention to the signs warning you that this is a busy road.

Turn **R** immediately after the bridge onto a lane signed Derwent Valley. Follow this road back to Fairholmes.

## Local knowledge

Ladybower Dam was built to create the reservoir that now provides water for Sheffield, Derby, Nottingham and Leicester. Finished in 1943, it filled the valley around the junction of the Rivers Derwent and Ashop with water, flooding the villages of Ashopton and Derwent. In very dry summers, you might be able to spot them.

During World War II, 617 Squadron – the Dambusters – used the valley's upper dams to practice their aim with Barnes Wallis' 'bouncing bombs' in preparation for their famous raids on German dams. There is a small museum on this theme in the west tower of the Derwent Dam.

## family riding

Ladybower is one of the most popular family cycling spots in the National Park. If you need to hire bikes, are looking for a bite to eat or want to feed the ducks, park at Fairholmes and follow the described route for as far as you feel able before making a U-turn and retracing your steps. **Note**, you will need to arrive early on busy days if you intend hiring a bike.

## making a day of it

Follow cycle paths south for a short distance from this ride and join the Ladybower route described on page 17.

# parsley hay

Route 3 // 15km

This is an easy ride, almost entirely off-road on smooth trails through the green countryside of the White Peak. Fairly short, it can be ridden in around an hour if you're quick, or a little longer if you take a more relaxed approach. The route runs south from Parsley Hay along the Tissington Trail, passing through a dramatic-looking cutting, past Hartington Station and into open countryside, with expansive views south over Derbyshire. Leaving the cycleway, the ride runs along roads for a short distance before swinging onto a wide track between fields. A short, fast descent, still on good, wide tracks, leads to the High Peak Trail, which leads back north to the Tissington Trail, and the car.

The start of the route at Parsley Hay is just off the A515 between Buxton and Ashbourne. It's signposted on the right, at the bottom of a dip in the road, on a long straight, about 10km after leaving the outskirts of Buxton.

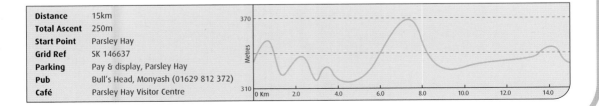

| Distance | 15km |
| --- | --- |
| Total Ascent | 250m |
| Start Point | Parsley Hay |
| Grid Ref | SK 146637 |
| Parking | Pay & display, Parsley Hay |
| Pub | Bull's Head, Monyash (01629 812 372) |
| Café | Parsley Hay Visitor Centre |

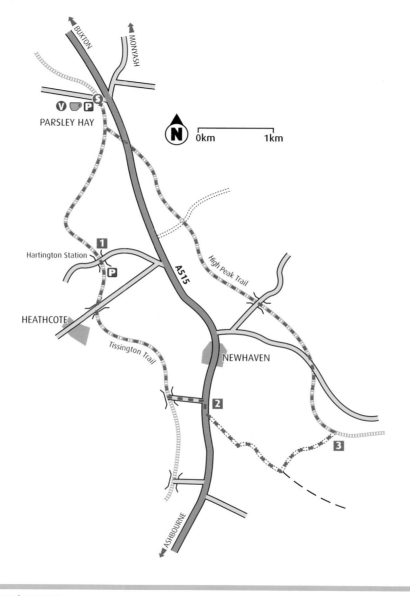

BUXTON

MONYASH

V ☕ P S
PARSLEY HAY

N   0km        1km

Hartington Station   **1**
P

High Peak Trail

A515

HEATHCOTE

Tissington Trail

NEWHAVEN

**2**

**3**

ASHBOURNE

From Parsley Hay, turn **L** along the cycleway to a wide fork and bear **R** along the Tissington Trail, soon passing through a big cutting.

**1** Pass Hartington station (an old signal box... we think) on your left. After 2.5km, just before crossing a road via a wooden-sided bridge, take a small track on the **L** to drop down to the road. Turn **L**.

**2** At the T-junction with the main road, turn **R** towards Ashbourne – take care, as cars hit high speeds along here – and then immediately turn **L** up a wide dirt track. Follow the track round to the **L** at the sharp bend and descend on a loose surface, trying not to be distracted by the views, to a crossroads of tracks (crosstracks, really).

**3** Turn **L** onto the High Peak Trail, and follow this back to Parsley Hay.

## famiLy RIDING

Cycleways, such as those taken by this route, get a big 'thumbs up' for riding with children. This route is no exception, although there is a short section of quiet road and then a busy road crossing to contend with.

## makinG a Day of it

You can keep going along the High Peak or Tissington Trails for as long as you like. Just remember, you'll have to ride the same distance back as you did on the way out! For more information on the trails, see page 99.

CROSSING OVERDALE BROOK, SHATTON

# six villages

route 4 // 11km

The Hope Valley is dominated by the often busy main road that runs along its base. It's easy to think of this as the defining feature of the valley and completely miss everything else that's there. Even those familiar with the area are often not aware of the many small hamlets and homesteads tucked away either by the river or around small wells and springs perched on the valley sides. This relatively short ride links the villages and hamlets of Hope, Aston, Thornhill, Bamford, Shatton and Brough, exploring the very heart of the valley. Most of the ride runs along very quiet lanes and byways. When it ventures off-road, the tracks are well surfaced – there's no need for the mountain bike here. There are two short sections along the main road, where, luckily, there is either a cycle lane or pavement.

The ride starts conveniently enough from the main car park in Hope, next to the toilets, opposite a café and by a pub – you could be excused for leaving the bikes on the bike rack!

The ride begins in Hope, which is fairly easy to find, as there's only one road, the A6187, running along the Hope Valley.

| Distance | 11km |
| --- | --- |
| Total Ascent | 230m |
| Start Point | Hope car park, near the Woodbine |
| Grid Ref | SK 167835 |
| Parking | Pay & display, Hope |
| Pub | The Cheshire Cheese Inn, Hope (01433 620 381) |
| Café | Woodbine Café, Hope (07778 113 882) |

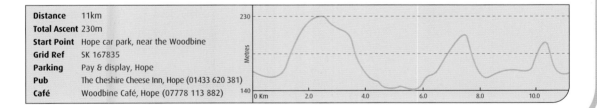

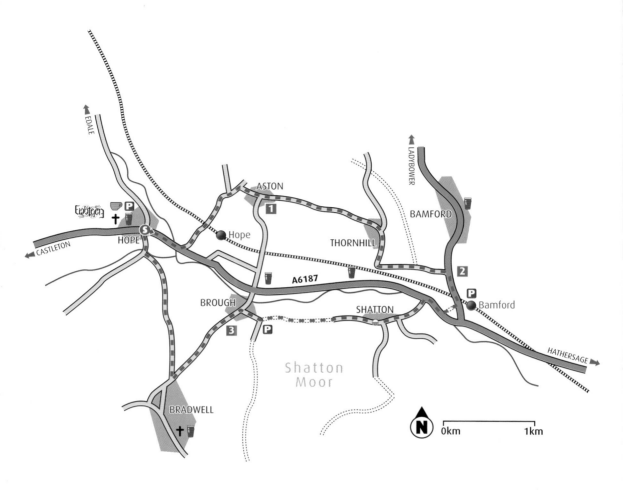

Turn **R** out of the car park down the main road, past the church and out of the village. Take the first **L**, signed Aston (no access to industrial estate), leaving the busy main road after what is – fortunately – a very short distance. Go under the railway bridge and a steady climb winds up the side of the valley. Follow the road as it dips, cutting into the valley floor where the sandstone and shale beds are exposed, and water is squeezed out, before emerging into the daylight once again in the centre of downtown Aston.

**1** Continue **SA** on Carr Lane, signed Unsuitable for motors, Thornhill. It's mostly downhill to the village. Turn **R** in the village for a fast downhill and turn **L** onto an un-signed and un-gated track 50m before the railway bridge and roughly 100m before the main road. Follow this track for a level kilometre, soon arriving at the main road to Bamford.

**2** Turn **R** down the main road, cross the railway line and take the next **R**, which cuts off a corner of the main valley road. Where the road ends, turn **R** across the footbridge over the River Derwent. It's probably best to continue along the pavement alongside the road due to the sheer volume of traffic here (in the summer, at least), but push if you do so. Head back up the valley for 100m and take the first **L**, over a bridge, to Shatton. Ride up into the village and take the first **R** to cross the ford, (by fair means or foul) and follow the quiet lane gently uphill. Keep **SA** where the lane turns uphill to the farms. Go more or less **SA** along the track, through the gate and downhill through a couple more gates to rejoin tarmac. Follow this **SA** down to the main road in Brough.

**3** Turn **L** at the main road, which gets a little narrow for the next 100m, and can be busy, so take care, especially if you have children along. After one kilometre, take the first **R** and wind uphill, then down again steeply. Turn **R** at the junction. Hopefully you are now back in Hope!

## LocaL knowLeDge
The Hope Valley runs east–west through the heart of the Peak District and marks the boundary between the Dark and White Peak. Sat as it is in the centre of the National Park, there's plenty to see and do. Head underground to the show caves, or uphill to Peveril Castle, both of which are to found at the head of the valley, near Castleton.

## famiLy RIDINg
This ride isn't too long, or too steep, although there are some sections of busy road, so older children should be fine on this ride.

## makINg a Day of it
A heritage trail begins in Bamford. Turn **L** half way along the track between Thornhill and Bamford to find it. It heads up towards Ladybower dam, where it slots neatly into the Ladybower ride that can be found on page 17.

# macclesfield forest

route 5 // 9km

Macclesfield Forest is a mysterious place; home to deer, buzzards, standing stones, earthworks and who knows what else. The forest bridleway is a fantastic, hilly challenge that loops around the wood and would be an ideal 'family' ride it if it wasn't on such a steep hillside. As it is, you'll need some low gears for the outward leg, although it's a very pleasant walk if you do have to push!, and good brakes and tyres for the way back – which is great fun and more than makes up for the effort put in on the climb. The majority of the ride, on the forest bridleway, doesn't really need an all-singing all-dancing mountain bike, but the loose and rocky section along Charity Lane certainly benefits from a bit of modern bike technology and a little off-road riding ability!

The starting point is conveniently equipped with picnic tables, or alternately head for the highly recommended Leather's Smithy Pub.

Macclesfield Forest lies in the south west corner of the Peak, between Buxton and Macclesfield, and just south of the main A537. One way to reach the forest is to descend from the high point of this road, near the Cat and Fiddle pub, towards Macclesfield for about 1km and then turn left onto a smaller road. Turn left at the pub, take the next right and head downhill into the forest when it comes into view.

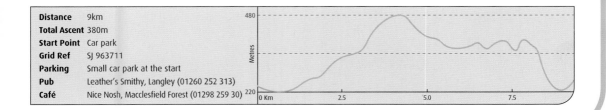

| Distance | 9km |
| Total Ascent | 380m |
| Start Point | Car park |
| Grid Ref | SJ 963711 |
| Parking | Small car park at the start |
| Pub | Leather's Smithy, Langley (01260 252 313) |
| Café | Nice Nosh, Macclesfield Forest (01298 259 30) |

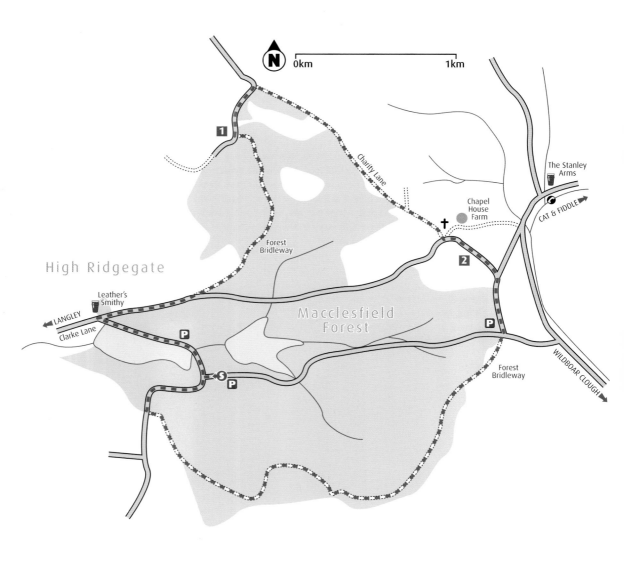

Leaving the car park, head back down dale towards a cross roads and turn **R**, (with the reservoir on your left), towards the Leather's Smithy public house. Turn **R** at the T-junction and follow the road steeply uphill. After 500m, turn **L** onto a hardpack trail up into the woods, following signs for the forest bridleway. The trail is steep at first but soon eases. Luckily, there is the odd bench here and there to rest upon! Keep on the main track to arrive at the tarmac road.

**1** Turn **R** uphill. The bad news is that this is the steepest part of the climb, while the good is that it's not too long. Just before the lane turns sharp left, turn **R** onto a track. This is Charity Lane, all very loose, rocky and challenging. Keep climbing to the summit and descend (with care) to Chapel House Farm – not one of England's biggest settlements... A right turn on the road leads back to the start. However, having climbed all the way up here, we're going to stay high a while longer – so continue **SA**.

**2** More pleasant uphill on tarmac leads to a T-junction near a car park. Continue **SA** over the road onto the forest bridleway. Follow the good hardpack trail as it undulates peacefully through the woods to a very fast descent down to the road. This will probably seem oh-so-short compared with the climb... Keep following the forest bridleway signs at the road, taking the first turning on the **R**. There's your car, on the right!

## Local knowledge

Wildlife spotting is usually a case of being in the right place at the right time, and being lucky. Spend some time in Macclesfield Forest and your chances of spotting something increase dramatically. A former Royal hunting forest, the area is home to a herd of red deer, which share their home with badgers and foxes. A heronry has been set up at Trentabank Reservoir (near the car park) and the odd otter can be seen around the banks of the forest's waterways.

## family riding

A beautiful forest, picnic tables, wildlife and some wide tracks – sounds good? Sadly the picnic area is at the bottom of the large hill mentioned in the main ride, so, unless you have very energetic children, you are perhaps better exploring the forest on foot.

CYCLING IN THE PEAK DISTRICT

CLIMBING PAST WINDGATHER ROCKS

# ɡoyt vaLLey

route 6 // 12km

The name "Goyt" has never struck us as a particularly attractive name. However, we've managed to put our prejudices to one side and visit the area on a few occasions – once for two years, but that's another story – and can confirm that you should never judge a valley by its rather unattractive name. The reservoirs at the start of this ride sit in a wooded valley, bordered on the south by heather-clad moorland, to the east and west by rolling countryside and to the north by deep valleys. The ride heads north along an easy trail through woodland, climbing up and out of the valley before swinging back south and climbing (for a long way) **up past Windgather Rocks for a sweeping descent back to the car. The further down the hill towards the reservoir you park, the longer this descent will be...**

There are two short sections of fairly tough rocky riding – one up and one downhill. Both are perfectly rideable, with a bit of willpower, but are only perhaps 100m long if you've got none and have to walk.

There are several lanes leading to the reservoirs in the Goyt Valley. We don't have space for detailed directions here, so take a road atlas – it's fairly easy to reach. However, the straightforward looking route heading due north from the A537 to Errwood Reservoir is one way only – south – so pick another way in!

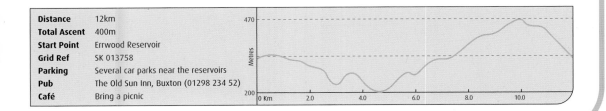

| Distance | 12km |
|---|---|
| Total Ascent | 400m |
| Start Point | Errwood Reservoir |
| Grid Ref | SK 013758 |
| Parking | Several car parks near the reservoirs |
| Pub | The Old Sun Inn, Buxton (01298 234 52) |
| Café | Bring a picnic |

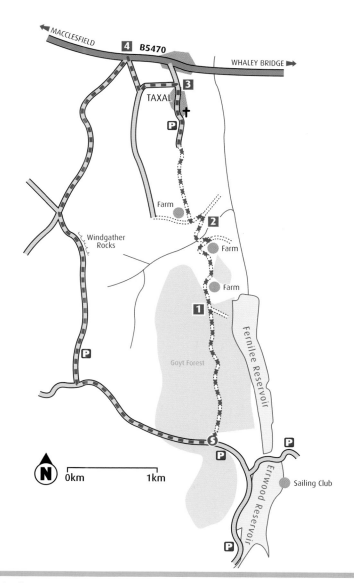

MACCLESFIELD

**4** B5470

WHALEY BRIDGE

**3**

TAXAL

P

Farm

**2**

Farm

Windgather
Rocks

Farm

**1**

Fernilee Reservoir

P

Goyt Forest

**S**
P

P

Errwood Reservoir

P

Sailing Club

N

0km          1km

P

From the dam separating the two reservoirs, cross to the side opposite the sailing club and take the lane heading uphill. Just after passing the end of the car park on the left, turn **R** through a gate onto a good track through the forest.

**1** Follow this track to a hairpin and ride **SA** across the bend to a gate. Go through this gate, following a sign to Taxal, and pass behind the buildings to a second gate. Keep following the obvious track, through another couple of gates, past a second farm and onto a short, tricky descent. At the T-junction with the better track, turn **L**.

**2** Follow the track around through gates to a T-junction at the top of the hill. Turn sharply **L** and follow the track along the brow of the hill with a wall to your right. Immediately before the buildings, turn **R** onto a good track and follow this **SA**, eventually onto tarmac and kinking to the left at the church, through the village of Taxal.

**3** Shortly after passing the 30mph limit signs, take the first lane on the **L**. Follow this around a sharp righthand bend and turn **R** up another lane. Climb steeply up and over the shoulder of the hill and descend to meet the main road. The expansive view out behind you on the climb should provide ample excuse for a breather...

**4** Turn **L** along the main road for, ooh, all of ten metres, and then turn **L** again onto a narrow lane. Climb (and climb and climb) to a crossroads. Turn **L** and climb past Windgather Rocks to a T-junction. Turn **L** and swoop (carefully, watching out for cars) down to the reservoirs and your car.

## Local knowledge

Unattractive though we may personally feel it to be, the name "Goyt" does not have any particularly unpleasant origins. The word "goyt" or "goit" is derived from the old English "gota", meaning stream or watercourse. This ride takes place relatively close to the source of the River Goyt, which rises on the moors above the valley and runs down to become a tributary of the River Mersey.

# tissington trail

route 7 // 12km

**A trip through the White Peak on well-surfaced trails and tarmac. Starting from the picturesque Peak village of Tissington, the ride follows the Tissington Trail as far as Alsop-en-le-Dale before climbing a gentle but long hill up a singletrack lane with ever-improving views out over the surrounding countryside. A fun road descent leads down to the Dog and Partridge pub and then either a return to your car on the Tissington Trail, or an extended road section to Ashbourne to pick up the Tissington Trail further south.**

The Tissington Trail follows the old Ashbourne-to-Buxton railway line. It was completed in 1899 and closed in 1967, becoming one of the first railway lines to be opened as a recreational trail four years later.

Tissington is easily reached, lying a little way north of Ashbourne, just off the A515. To find the Tissington Trail, head west out of the village and the car park is tucked away on the right.

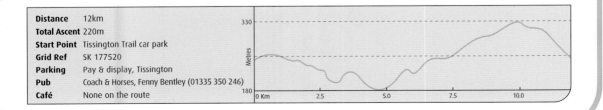

| | | |
|---|---|---|
| **Distance** | 12km | |
| **Total Ascent** | 220m | |
| **Start Point** | Tissington Trail car park | |
| **Grid Ref** | SK 177520 | |
| **Parking** | Pay & display, Tissington | |
| **Pub** | Coach & Horses, Fenny Bentley (01335 350 246) | |
| **Café** | None on the route | |

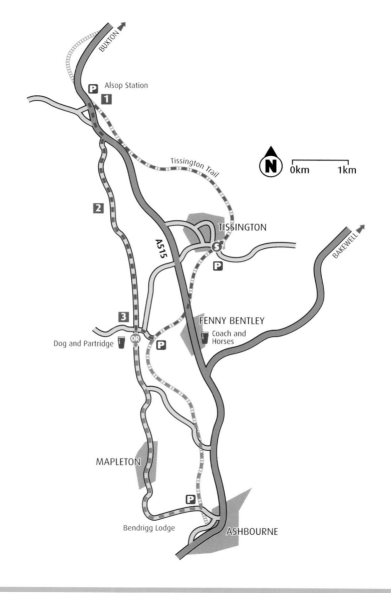

BUXTON

P Alsop Station

1

Tissington Trail

N 0km 1km

2

A515

TISSINGTON

S

P

BAKEWELL

3

FENNY BENTLEY

Coach and
Horses

OR

Dog and Partridge P

MAPLETON

P

Bendrigg Lodge ASHBOURNE

Turn **L** from the car park (as you face the trail) onto the Tissington Trail to follow the old railway line for just over 4km to Alsop car park (small car park on your left with a small sign at the far end that tells you you're in Alsop-en-le-Dale).

**1** Leave the trail and ride through the car park and up the short lane to the main road. Turn **L** along the main road. (Careful – it can be fast and busy!). Take the second lane on the **R** – a singletrack road on the top of the small rise.

**2** Follow this road uphill with ever-improving views. Pass through the gates (don't let the cows out!) and descend to the Dog and Partridge pub at a crossroads.

**3** Turn **L** and then **R** down a dead-end lane as the road swings to the left. Follow this lane to its end at a car park and continue straight through the car park to the Tissington Trail. Turn **L** and follow the trail back to Tissington.

**Optional route:** Continue **SA** at the crossroads. After 1km, turn **R**, signed Mapleton and Ashbourne. Follow the lane downhill through Mapleton and round to the left. Just before reaching the houses at Ashbourne, turn **L** into Mapleton Lane car park. Go through the car park and turn **L** onto the Tissington Trail.

Before you leave Mapleton Lane, turn **R** on the trail and have a look at the impressive old railway tunnel at the far end of the car park. This has had a "soundtrack" added to it to recreate the sounds of a working railway line.

## Local knowledge

If you are in the area at the end of May, head into the village of Tissington itself to see the annual well-dressing ceremony. This tradition, which is hundreds of years old, does not involve one's Sunday best, but is the act of decorating the local water supply. A possible origin for this practice comes from the fourteenth century, when the village of Tissington, having escaped infection by the plague, put their lucky escape down to the purity of the water coming from their wells.

## family riding

Tissington is a lovely village and the Tissington Trail is a lovely cycleway. If you want to keep your children off the road, stick to the Tissington Trail for as long as you like before retracing your steps (personally, we'd head north along it – the views are better).

# CHELMORTON

route 8 // 19km

**This ride is undoubtably best ridden on a clear day, as it takes you on a loop around a high limestone plateau and it would be a shame to miss the views. Being high and exposed, it can also get rather bleak and windy in bad weather. Check the forecast in advance, pick your day accordingly and you'll be well rewarded!**

Starting from Parsley Hay Visitor Centre, the ride heads out along the High Peak Trail for a few kilometres of easy dirt track. At the end of the trail, the ride moves on to tarmac and heads for the village of Chelmorton (and a pub if you want to stop for a breather) before climbing steeply out above the village and descending gently towards Monyash. From here, a road climb (groan) leads back to Parsley Hay and its sandwich shop.

Parsley Hay has a visitor centre, sandwich shop, bike hire, toilets and drinking-water tap.

The start of the route at Parsley Hay is just off the A515 between Buxton and Ashbourne. It's signposted on the right, at the bottom of a dip in the road (on a long straight) about 10km after leaving the outskirts of Buxton.

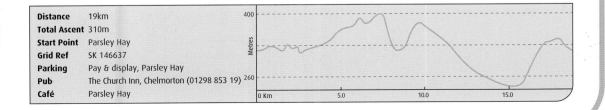

| | |
|---|---|
| **Distance** | 19km |
| **Total Ascent** | 310m |
| **Start Point** | Parsley Hay |
| **Grid Ref** | SK 146637 |
| **Parking** | Pay & display, Parsley Hay |
| **Pub** | The Church Inn, Chelmorton (01298 853 19) |
| **Café** | Parsley Hay |

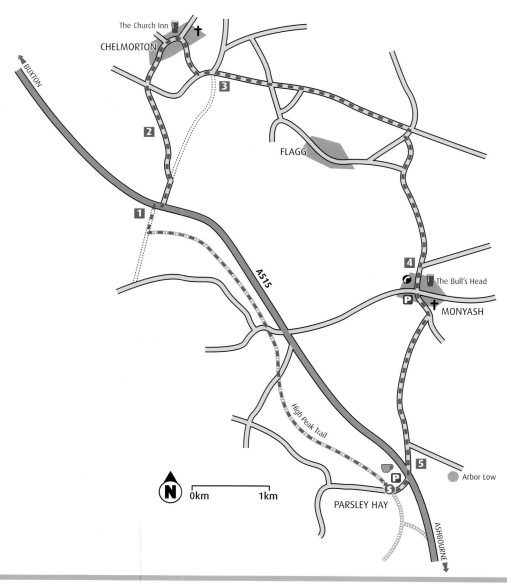

The Church Inn

CHELMORTON

BUXTON

FLAGG

A515

The Bull's Head

MONYASH

High Peak Trail

Arbor Low

N

0km          1km

PARSLEY HAY

ASHBOURNE

Turn **R** along the High Peak Trail from Parsley Hay. Follow the cycleway until you reach its end at a gate and T-junction. Turn **R** and ride uphill towards the main road.

**1** At the road, you could duke it out with the cars and lorries, but it would make more sense to take the Pennine Bridleway. Turn **R** along this and follow it to the end of the fence that separates you from the road. Cross the main road and go **SA** down the lane opposite.

**2** Follow this lane to a crossroads and go **SA** into the village of Chelmorton. Follow the road through the village and round to the **R** at the far end. (The road straight ahead is marked as a no-through road and leads to a conveniently located pub). Climb steeply out of Chelmorton and follow the road **SA** (still climbing) at the junction.

**3** Go **SA** over the crossroads and descend the undulating road with magnificent views ahead. Take the third **R** (not counting the crossroads you went straight ahead at), signed Monyash and Flagg. Turn **L** after 200m, this time signed only to Monyash and follow the road into the village.

**4** At the crossroads by the Bull's Head pub (on your left, across the green), go **SA** up Rakes Road, signed Newhaven and Youlgreave. Follow this road until you reach a T-junction with the busy A515.

**5** Turn **L** along the A515 for about 20 metres and then **R** down the minor road. (Essentially, go **SA** over the A515.)

Turn **R** almost immediately, following signs back to Parsley Hay.

## Local knowledge

Sometimes referred to as the 'Stonehenge of the Peak District', Arbor Low, a Neolithic/Early Bronze Age stone circle, lies just off this route near Monyash. Unlike other circles, the stones forming Arbor Low lie flat on the ground and it is not known whether they ever stood upright. It has been suggested that they once did and that early Christians pulled them over in order to 'de-sanctify' the site.

## family riding

The ride begins on the High Peak Trail at Parsley Hay cycle hire and café, and is thus perfectly suited to short family rides of whatever length you chose. Head north towards the end of the High Peak Trail, or head south to the junction of the High Peak and Tissington Trails. For more information on these cycleways, see page 99.

## making a day of it

The Parsley Hay route on page 25 shares the same start and finish as this ride, but heads south rather than north. The two could be joined for a full day's riding.

# mIDDLetoN top

ROUte 9 // 22km

**Roughly three-quarters off-road, this is a good, easy-going circuit, albeit a relatively long one with a fair amount of climbing. The riding is never difficult, and the climbs, although long, are not too steep and are on good, well-surfaced tracks.**

Leaving Middleton Top, where you can hire bikes, if necessary, the route heads quite literally up the High Peak Trail to Hopton Top, where it turns off the trail onto bridleways running through fields and along good tracks to Grangemill. Roads and wide tracks wind through the White Peak towards Gotham, from where the High Peak Trail can be rejoined and followed back to the start.

If you don't fancy the full 22km ride, you can turn this into a great 17km loop by starting at the car park near Gotham, riding down the High Peak Trail to Hopton Top and then turning onto the bridleway described at **2** in the directions.

To find Middleton Top, head out of Matlock Bath, go through Cromford and then turn right towards Middleton. Middleton Top is signed from Matlock Bath.

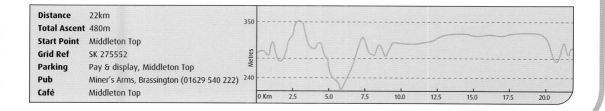

| Distance | 22km |
|---|---|
| Total Ascent | 480m |
| Start Point | Middleton Top |
| Grid Ref | SK 275552 |
| Parking | Pay & display, Middleton Top |
| Pub | Miner's Arms, Brassington (01629 540 222) |
| Café | Middleton Top |

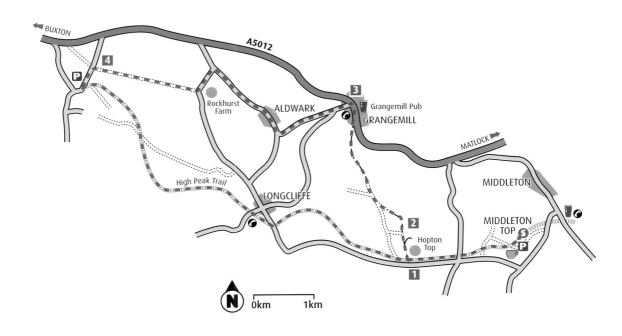

Leave Middleton Top by turning **L** onto the High Peak Trail, climbing away from Matlock.

**1** After about 2km, the trail runs parallel to the road, which is on the left and below you. As the road and trail converge, in height, pass through the gate at Hopton Top, continue past the building and then turn **R** through a gate onto a grassy bridleway, signed Grangemill Head.

**2** Follow the bridleway across the field and through gates until it becomes a good track. Go **SA** when the track swings left, onto a fine fast bridleway to join a larger track. Follow this, turning **L** and then downhill, ignoring a left branch up towards the farm.

After a descent and a climb, go through some gates and turn **R** onto a bridleway signed Grangemill. Good singletrack leads through a field to the village of Grangemill.

**3** Turn **L** towards Longcliffe, turning **R** after 150m up a narrow lane towards Aldwark. Head uphill and go **SA** through the village, taking the lane to the **L** after approximately 1.5km. Follow this lane for 300m until it swings left at Rockhurst Farm. Turn **R** here onto a farm track and follow this to the road.

**4** Turn **L** along the road. Ignore the first track on the left (which passes under a high stone bridge) and ride to the top of the short climb. Just beyond the 'summit', turn **L** back onto the High Peak Trail and follow this back to your car. You'll be re-tracing your steps for the last few kilometres.

## Local knowledge

Don't worry if you find the going tough – the climb up to Hopton Top, at 1 in 14, was the steepest section of railway line in Britain regularly used by conventional steam engines. Even they occasionally ran out of steam (ho ho) and had to be helped to the top. Don't worry too much though, as the gradient has now been made more cycle-friendly and is no longer as steep as it once was!

## family riding

Riders of any age can tackle the sections of this route on the High Peak Trail. Younger riders might struggle with the incline towards Hopton Top, although they'll probably love the return journey! See page 99 for more information on the High Peak Trail.

# Hathersage

## route 10 // 20km

**For the average tourist, the Hope Valley has Castleton at one end – with nothing much to do other than mill around and look at the show caves – and Hathersage at the other – more milling, but no show caves. Stop in one village, and then drive to the other, cup of tea, slice of cake, home, same again next half term?**

Now if you are a bit fed up with the shops – and let's face it, they all sell the same things, except, of course, the excellent shop that sold you this book – why not try this cycle ride? Any old bike will do, as the route is mostly on tarmac, and mainly quiet stretches at that. Starting in a valley and avoiding the main road will inevitably lead to some fierce hill climbs, but a plethora of hamlets and farmsteads, hidden valleys, great views and varied flora and fauna make this a very rewarding leisure ride – pub included at the half way point.

An alternative extension to this route climbs from Abney before dropping to Offerton and Highlow Halls to rejoin the return leg – worthwhile if you need to loose the calories. This option adds great views and a taste of the awesome mountain biking in the region. This predominately off-road extension is best completed on a mountain bike.

The ride starts from the large pay and display car park, in the centre of Hathersage, opposite the swimming pool. The car park is signed off the B6001, which is the road from the centre of the village, towards the station on the way to Grindleford.

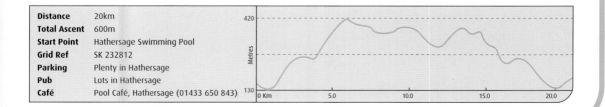

| Distance | 20km |
|---|---|
| Total Ascent | 600m |
| Start Point | Hathersage Swimming Pool |
| Grid Ref | SK 232812 |
| Parking | Plenty in Hathersage |
| Pub | Lots in Hathersage |
| Café | Pool Café, Hathersage (01433 650 843) |

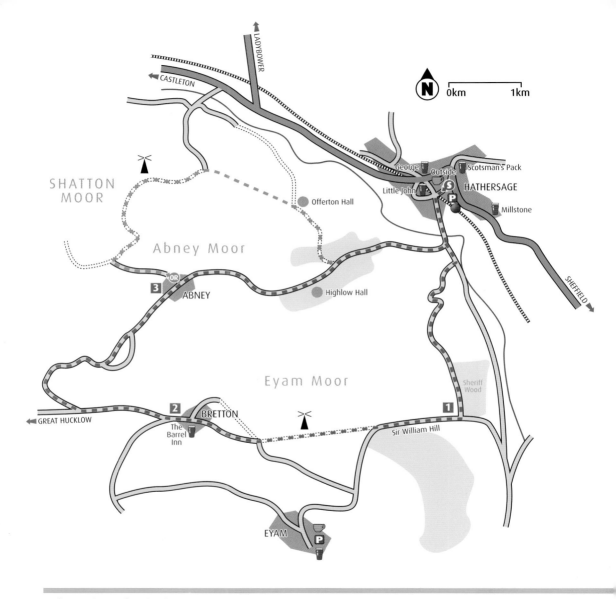

Start from the large pay and display car park in the centre of Hathersage, opposite the open-air swimming pool.

Head **R** from the car park and turn **L** onto the main road. Follow this downhill, over the river and past the Plough Inn and the turning to Abney. Continue **SA** for a further 200 metres after this turning and then turn **R** onto an unsigned lane. This is what we guys call a quiet lane. Follow this lane uphill to Hazelford and follow the steepening incline uphill into the delightful Sheriff Wood. There's even a bit of a downhill here!

**1** At the T-junction, turn **R** and climb up onto Eyam Moor. This is Sir William Hill, and a right b*gger he is too! Go **SA** as the road swings left, onto the broken gravel and hardpack track, heading towards the summit of Sir William. Pass the mast and, after about 1.5km, rejoin tarmac. Keep going **SA** to the tiny village of Bretton, and the pub we promised you, the tucked-away Barrel Inn.

**2** Head **SA**, taking the first **R** fork in the road, (ignoring the road off to Foolow). Head **SA** along the road towards Great Hucklow, the significant other of the diminutive Little Hucklow. Soon after entering the woods and before descending to the village, fork **R** uphill, signed Gliding Club and Abney. Follow the road around Hucklow Edge, keeping **SA** all the way to the hamlet of Abney.

**3** Go **SA** through Abney, then drop pleasantly into the woods – picturesque in bluebell season – and keep descending past Highlow Hall to the main road by the Plough. Turn **L** and retrace your steps to the finish.

**Optional Route:** We'd recommend a mountain bike for this option.

From the 'centre' of Abney, turn **L** uphill into the wilderness of Abney Moor. At the roadhead, turn **R** and follow the rutted bridleway uphill, keeping to the track as it makes its way leftwards, to meet a gate.

Go through the gate and head along the lane, through the puddles, past the mast and downhill on the track. Where the track meets tarmac on a left-hand corner, go **R** through a gate onto a bridleway through the field. Keep **SA**, soon picking up a good bridleway downhill, which can be muddy. All too soon the fun ends, and the mountain biking gives way to tarmac at a gate just above at Offerton Hall.

Turn **R** uphill and follow the lane, pleasantly descending to rejoin the main route just past Highlow Hall.

# family RIDING
Head elsewhere. There's not a vast amount of child-friendly riding in this area. The closest family riding spot is Ladybower Reservoir.

heading towards hen cloud

# tHe ROacHes

ROUte 11 // 19km

**The Peak District is an incredibly varied place. Whereas some national parks, such as the Lake District and the Yorkshire Dales, have one overriding image** (lakes and trees vs sheep and limestone walls)**, the Peak has several. Made up as it is of several different counties, two strikingly different geologies, a variety of geographies and the influence of human impact, it has many different faces – not just those of the Dark and White Peaks. These faces range from gritstone crags and wild moors to industrial relics and from rolling woodland and limestone dales to picturesque villages.**

This ride takes the cyclist through layers of Peak District landscape, to the east of the Dane Valley, and under the shadow of the Roaches cliffs. The pink gritstone rock makes for distinctive local buildings, while the ride varies between farmland and moorland, giving it interest at every bend.

The ride traverses under the Roaches crags, a short off-road section soon rejoins tarmac for a long downhill – almost down to the River Dane, before a traverse around the rolling fields and woods of rural Staffordshire, leading to a final stiff climb back to the café.

This ride starts from the Roaches Tea Rooms, under the popular climbing and walking area of The Roaches. There is ample parking all along the lane, that soon fills up on sunny Sundays. A park and ride scheme runs in the summer! The area is found off the A53 Leek to Buxton road. Turn off the main road signed to Upper Hulme, follow the narrow lane into the hamlet, turning off again to cross the stream and head up to the parking.

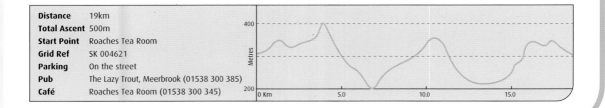

| Distance | 19km |
|---|---|
| Total Ascent | 500m |
| Start Point | Roaches Tea Room |
| Grid Ref | SK 004621 |
| Parking | On the street |
| Pub | The Lazy Trout, Meerbrook (01538 300 385) |
| Café | Roaches Tea Room (01538 300 345) |

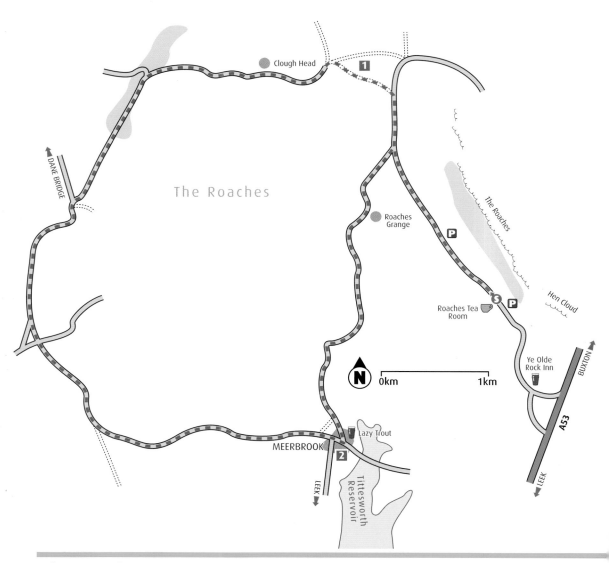

The Roaches

Clough Head

Roaches Grange

The Roaches

Hen Cloud

DANE BRIDGE

**1**

**2**

P

Roaches Tea
Room

S

P

Ye Olde
Rock Inn

BUXTON

A53

LEEK

Lazy Trout

MEERBROOK

LEEK

Tittesworth
Reservoir

N

0km          1km

From the café, head up the valley, passing under the crag on the right. Continue **SA**, passing a lane off to the left. Fork **L** onto a grassy track, signed Clough Head, just past an old gate on the road, which is often closed, and 250m before a new wooden gate, which is always closed.

**1** Follow this grassy/muddy lane to a road by a gate (only short to push if it is too muddy). Go through this gate and head downhill past Clough Head Farm. Keep **SA** to a T-junction, turn **L** and keep **SA** again, following the road for about three kilometres, before turning **L** again down a lane signed Meerbrook. Continue **SA** over the crossroads, following the road to Meerbrook.

**2** Upon entering the hamlet, turn **L** just before the Lazy Trout pub and follow the lane uphill, signed Roche Grange. Ride through Roche Grange and then steeply uphill for a short distance to arrive back on the lane under the Roaches crag. Turn **R** and head back to the café.

## Local knowledge
Somewhat bizarrely, the area around the Roaches used to be home to around 50 wallabies. The Peak District Wallabies, along with a yak, escaped from a nearby private zoo in around 1940 and managed to breed and live in the area until the 1990s, when they were thought to die out. However, they have done that a few times, so keep an eye out...

entering miller's dale on a damp day

# Litton

*Route 12 // 23km*

**This big ride traces a long loop around the heart of the limestone plateaux. Dry dales, miles of stone walls, green pastures and idyllic villages and hamlets. The ride is good in that, unlike many rides of this length in the Peak District, it doesn't have too many hills. It is even possible to skip the steep descent into and out of Miller's Dale if you feel tired towards the end of the ride and need to save some energy, although you'd miss the impressive Raven Crag.**

Off-road bikes are needed for this route, although it is essentially all on quiet lanes. The flora and fauna of the Peak litter the ride at every turn; the thread of a dale running down from Peak Forest to join the Wye at Miller's Dale is a birdwatchers' and botanists' heaven, while the Wye itself is home to herons, dippers, kingfishers, coots, moorhens, dabchicks and perhaps one of Britain's least-spotted animals – the otter. For the more sedate, the Red Lion in Litton serves up another of Britain's most special animals – The Pint.

Litton is a one-horse town, and that horse can be found on the main road through the village, drinking at Red Lion pub on the right as you approach the village on Mires Lane. Litton is signed left off the main A623 Stoney Middleton to Peak Forest Road, 300 metres after Wardlow Mires as you approach from Stoney.

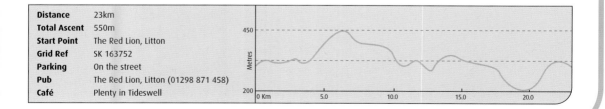

| Distance | 23km |
|---|---|
| Total Ascent | 550m |
| Start Point | The Red Lion, Litton |
| Grid Ref | SK 163752 |
| Parking | On the street |
| Pub | The Red Lion, Litton (01298 871 458) |
| Café | Plenty in Tideswell |

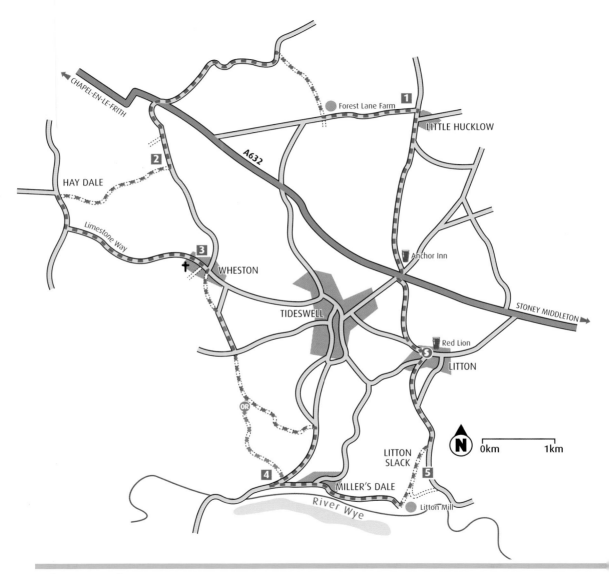

Forest Lane Farm

LITTLE HUCKLOW

CHAPEL-EN-LE-FRITH

A632

HAY DALE

Limestone Way

Anchor Inn

STONEY MIDDLETON

WHESTON

TIDESWELL

Red Lion

LITTON

LITTON SLACK

MILLER'S DALE

River Wye

Litton Mill

0km    1km

From the front door of the Red Lion in Litton, turn **R** and head **SA** down the narrow lane towards Tideswell. After 400 metres, turn **R** along a slightly narrower lane which meets the main A623 at the Anchor Inn. It's too early for a break, I'm afraid, so cross the road and take Castleton Lane running off **L** from the front of the inn. Follow the road past a very round wood on the left and keep going, crossing the workings of High Rake. Follow the road as it descends and then climbs, before taking the next **L**, signed Peak Forest.

**1** Follow the road for a little over 1km, turning **R** onto a good hardpack lane just after Forest Lane Farm. Follow the lane, squeezing through the well-signed narrow section. It's very rideable, even in the wintertime. On meeting tarmac, turn **L** and follow the lane down to the main road. This is loosely along the lines of the Roman road – Batham Gate.

Go **SA** over the main road and continue along the quiet lane on the Limestone Way. Ignoring the first lane off to the right, pass Limestone Way Farm and then turn **R** onto the (signed) Limestone Way.

**2** Take care here – this is mountain biking terrain. The lane drops steeply, the limestone rocks can be slippery and it can be muddy after bad weather or in the depths of winter, although it remains perfectly rideable. The lane drops into the base of the dry valley of Hay Dale, and climbs easily back out to the road. Turn **L**, and after 300m take the first **L**, dropping back into the aforementioned dale, and climbing out once more. Keep following the road to drop pleasantly into the delightful village of Wheston.

**3** Pass the village cross and the grand Wheston Hall Farm before turning **R** along the Limestone Way, up a good track. Quickly meeting tarmac, keep **SA**. At a crossroads, go **SA** onto a rutted track, turning **L** at a vague T-junction, before the main track begins to descend steeply.

**Optional Route:** Hardcore mountain bikers may want to keep on the main track and enjoy the steep, tough descent, rejoining the main route at **4**.

At the road, turn **R** and follow it steeply downhill.

**4** Reaching the main road, turn **R** and immediately back **L** into Miller's Dale, soon passing the Angler's Rest (or in our case, the Cyclists' Rest). Follow the delightful River Wye – the resurgence for many of the hidden streams that underlie much of the dry valleys and dales we have been traversing earlier in the day. At Litton Mill, turn up **L** just before the gates down to the mill; head up steeply on tarmac, then **SA** up a track to a gate. Go through this and (push) your bike up the dry dale to the top. The tigers amongst you will, of course, ride this section, the canny will take the zig off to the **R** after 50m, and then zag back up to the gate.

**5** At the top, go through the gate, through the hamlet of Litton Slack, **SA** and up to the T-junction. Turn **L**, down the lane, heading **L** at the fork, and then drop into Litton, turning **R** back to the start.

# Longstone edge & eyam

Route 13 // 18km

A great ride with some good views, fun riding and a fair amount of not-too-tricky off-road. This ride does, however, tackle some long climbs and runs along busy roads for a short distance, so it is better suited to more confident riders. Starting in the picturesque village of Great Longstone, the ride climbs steeply up the lane onto Longstone Edge. The views from this climb are among the best in the Peak. A little more tarmac-bashing leads to the first section of off-road riding – a gravel and mud track to the village of Eyam and a tea stop if needed. From Eyam, a tricky rocky track runs downhill to Stoney Middleton. Watch out for this track in the damp – you need to be on-form to stay upright on the wet and slimy limestone. From Stoney, the route follows a short section of busy road to Calver Crossroads and then takes a stone track to climb back up onto Longstone Edge for a rattling descent back down to Great Longstone.

The ride starts from the centre of the village. Get the road atlas out and follow signs to Great Longtone, find a place to park and start riding!

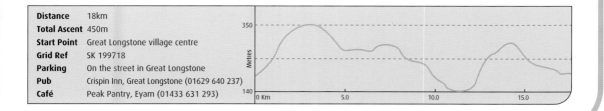

| Distance | 18km |
|---|---|
| Total Ascent | 450m |
| Start Point | Great Longstone village centre |
| Grid Ref | SK 199718 |
| Parking | On the street in Great Longstone |
| Pub | Crispin Inn, Great Longstone (01629 640 237) |
| Café | Peak Pantry, Eyam (01433 631 293) |

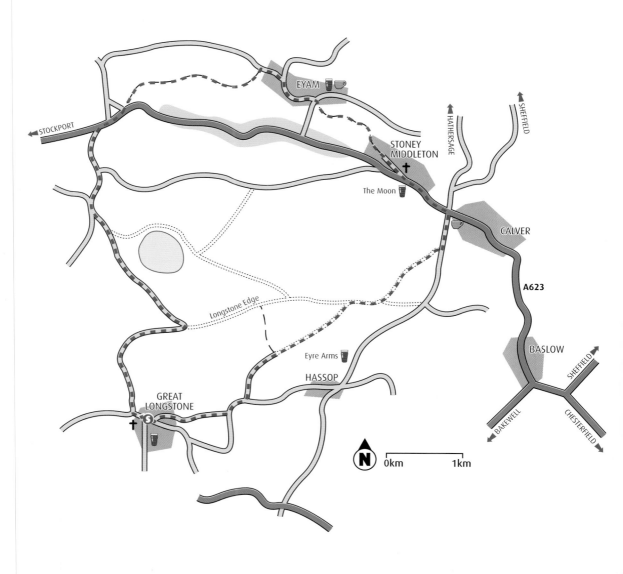

STOCKPORT

EYAM

HATHERSAGE

SHEFFIELD

STONEY
MIDDLETON

The Moon

CALVER

A623

Longstone Edge

BASLOW

Eyre Arms

HASSOP

SHEFFIELD

GREAT
LONGSTONE

BAKEWELL

CHESTERFIELD

N

0km    1km

Climb the main road through Great Longstone in the direction of Monsal Head, turning **R** up a lane towards Longstone Edge just after passing the village green. The ever-improving view should help take your mind off the climbing!

**1** Follow the road round to the left to a T-junction. Turn **R** and ride to the next T-junction. Take care here – this is a busy road. Turn **R** and then take the second **L** (after about 500m). Immediately after leaving the main road, turn **R** onto a dark grey dirt track bordered by drystone walls. This track initially runs parallel to the main road and is signed Unsuitable for Motor Vehicles.

**2** This track spits you out in the village of Eyam, where, if you want them, you'll find a couple of village shops, café and a pub. As the track ends, turn **R** and follow the lane downhill into the centre of the village, keeping **L** at the road junction in the centre. Don't turn right and start to descend!.

**3** Turn **R** up a narrow lane between houses about 10m before the tea rooms. Follow this road to its end and continue **SA**, keeping to the **L** onto another track signed Unsuitable for Motor Vehicles.

This track begins on tarmac before moving on to a fairly tricky downhill section. Take it easy if you're not used to riding off-road – the slick limestone can spit you off your bike without any warning! Things ease after a gate. Stick to the track until you reach tarmac at Stoney village. Keep going **SA** down the tarmac lane to a T-junction. Turn left (in effect, continue **SA**) and follow the lane through the village to the main road by the excellent Moon Pub.

**4** Turn **R** along the main road. Be careful – this is a busy road, although there is a 40mph speed restriction. At the crossroads after 1km, turn **R**. Climb past the second road on the left and then turn **R** soon afterwards, through a gate onto a gravel track.

**5** Climb around the zig zags and keep going up (and up) until the track levels out. Keep **L** at the fork and continue to a large junction of tracks. Turn **R** and keep on the main track and turn **L** just after passing under some pylons. If you start to climb steeply with a large quarry on your right, you've gone too far. Descend the rough track into Rowland. As the track turns to tarmac, keep going **SA** and ride through Rowland to a T-junction.

Turn **R** and follow the road back to Great Longstone.

## LocaL knowLeDçe

In 1665, the Black Death arrived in the village of Eyam (pronounced 'eem') in a bundle of flea-infested cloth sent from London. When the cloth was hung out to dry, the fleas were released and plague began to spread through the village. The people of Eyam took the decision to quarantine themselves, staying within the confines of their village. Food and other goods were left above Eyam and payment was left in vinegar-soaked holes nearby, or in Mompesson's Well, where the water could wash it clean. Over then next 14 months, around 250 people died in the village, but the actions of those who lived there ensured that the plague did not spread beyond their parish.

Interestingly, it is now known that some of the village population were naturally immune to the disease.

B6050

7

Oran
Publi
Permis
Public
Cycle ro
Wheelcha
picnic area
Jigsaw line
Jigsaw piece
River
Woodland
Emergency te
Picnic site
Toilets
Step

Ranger's office
WC

P

P

P

P

Lower
Reservoir

# Linacre Woods

route 14 // 11km

In the dry this is a fantastic route, almost entirely off-road, mixing up wide, open tracks with twisty stuff in the woods. Hardly ever flat, this does mean that you spend a bit of time climbing, but it also means that there are plenty of downhills. Watch out, as some of them are steep! The ride is worth doing in both directions, being equally good either way round. Of course, at the end of one loop you could always do a U-turn and ride it twice!

Unfortunately, the best bits of this ride are only the best bits when the ground is bone dry. So, unless you can ride a bike in thick mud, can happily drag clay-encrusted bikes up steep slopes and have an unshakeable belief that any ride is a good ride, wait until summer before attempting this route.

Linacre Woods is signposted off the B6050, between Cutthorpe and Prathall.

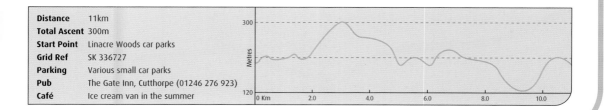

| Distance | 11km |
|---|---|
| Total Ascent | 300m |
| Start Point | Linacre Woods car parks |
| Grid Ref | SK 336727 |
| Parking | Various small car parks |
| Pub | The Gate Inn, Cutthorpe (01246 276 923) |
| Café | Ice cream van in the summer |

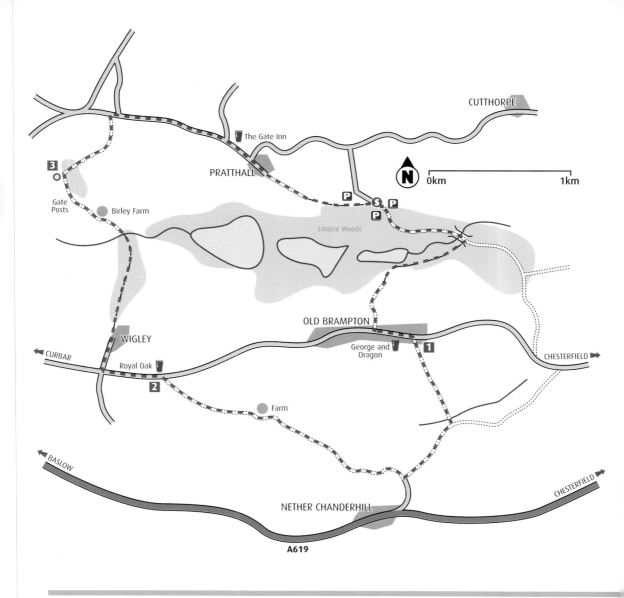

CUTTHORPE

The Gate Inn

PRATTHALL

**3**
○
Gate
Posts

Birley Farm

Linacre Woods

**N**
0km        1km

**P**
**S**
**P**
**P**

OLD BRAMPTON

WIGLEY

◀ CURBAR

Royal Oak

**2**

George and
Dragon

**1**

CHESTERFIELD ▶

Farm

◀ BASLOW

CHESTERFIELD ▶

NETHER CHANDERHILL

**A619**

Regardless of which car park you start this ride from, head along the lane dropping towards the reservoirs. As the road turns sharply to the right, go **SA** onto a dirt track and continue descending into the woods. Turn sharp **R** just after the bridge onto a wide bridleway, soon climbing out of the trees. Follow the track up through the trees and out into the open, eventually meeting a road. Turn **L** and head down the road for a short distance before taking a bridleway on the **R**.

**1** Descend to the stream, and take the track **R** at the next T-junction. Follow this uphill, turning back **R** downhill where the track turns to tarmac. Descend steeply past the buildings and follow the wide track onwards and upwards, bearing **L** at the next farm.

**2** At the road, turn **L**, and then take the next **R**, signed Wigley. Follow this lane and bear **L** by the stone toadstool down the often muddy bridleway – remember what we said about riding in the summer! Follow the twisty, rooty and steep descent, via any one of its many permutations, down to the stream. Cross this and climb steeply up to Birley Farm as the path turns to a wide strip of mown grass. Head **L** along the tarmac, through the fine gates.

**3** Turn **R** opposite the pond and go through the gate onto a bridleway through the trees. Follow this **SA** onto a track and head uphill towards the road, keeping left at the farm. Turn **R** at the road and follow it down past The Gate Inn, taking the next turning on the **R**. Follow this through the houses and continue **SA** through gates as the road becomes track and then runs through a grassy field. Follow it alongside the woods and back to the reservoir access road.

# castleton

route 15 // 16km

**Climb a road that fell down a hill, cruise around a high plateau, drop into and climb out of a picturesque dale and then plummet back down to the tourist hotspot of Castleton.**

This ride begins by climbing a steep hill on a collapsed road. It's a hard way to start a ride, but gets you up high, leaving you to enjoy the views and revel in the knowledge that there's an equally long downhill to come. A brief section on a fairly busy road leads to an easy off-road track through a field. This, in turn, leads to another track, which is often full of unavoidable puddles, and then to a fun descent into Perry Dale. Look out for the resident family of buzzards! The climb back out is fairly long, but runs through pleasant countryside and is easy enough. Once at the top, a fast, wide track leads back down towards Castleton to the road, where there are two options: a fast swoop down the road or a loose, rocky and technical rattle down Pindale. We'd recommend the road route – it's fast and fun and more in keeping with the rest of the ride. The off-road alternative, whilst fun, is tricky, with some big rocks and loose ground – perhaps best left to mountain bikers.

The ride begins from the main car park by the only mini roundabout in the village in the centre of Castleton, Castleton is well signed and lies on the A6187 at the end of the Hope Valley.

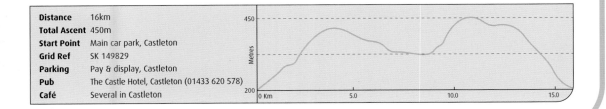

| | |
|---|---|
| **Distance** | 16km |
| **Total Ascent** | 450m |
| **Start Point** | Main car park, Castleton |
| **Grid Ref** | SK 149829 |
| **Parking** | Pay & display, Castleton |
| **Pub** | The Castle Hotel, Castleton (01433 620 578) |
| **Café** | Several in Castleton |

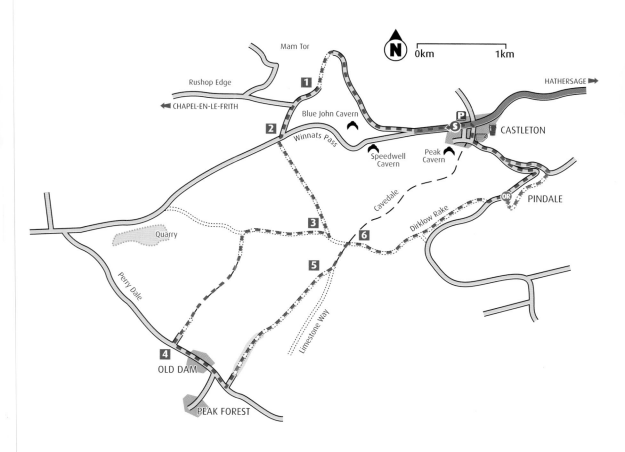

Mam Tor

Rushop Edge

**◄ CHAPEL-EN-LE-FRITH**

**1**

Blue John Cavern

**2**

Winnats Pass

Speedwell
Cavern

Peak
Cavern

**HATHERSAGE ►**

**P**

**S**

**CASTLETON**

Cavedale

Dirklow Rake

**OR**

**PINDALE**

**3**

**6**

Quarry

**5**

Perry Dale

Limestone Way

**4**

**OLD DAM**

**PEAK FOREST**

0km    1km

N

From the main Castleton car park, go back to the main road and turn **R**, heading up the valley. Follow the road out of Castleton, keeping right at the fork, and soon start to climb. Keep going as the road swings back left, through a gate and continues to climb on broken tarmac.

**1** At the top, go **SA** to the main road. Turn **L** (essentially **SA**), following the road round the corners.

**2** Soon after passing a road on the left, turn **L** through the first gate you reach in the fence onto a wide tarmac track (if you reach the buildings, you've missed it). Follow the track through a gate and, as it bends to the left, turn **R** through another gate.

**Shortcut:** You could continue straight ahead here, meeting the route at point **6** in 200m. This will miss the descent and climb out of Perry Dale, but save at least half an hour.

**3** Follow the track through two gates and, as the track bends right, turn **L** through a small gate onto a signed bridleway. After a second gate, head uphill slightly and follow the vague track **SA**. Keep to this track as it runs alongside the wall to a wide gate into a field, where the track disappears. Continue through the gate and across the field to a gate in the far side (too far downhill to be seen initially). Go through the gate, past the farm and turn **L** at the T-junction.

**4** In the village, turn **L** at the junction by the grass roundabout. Follow the lane uphill and take the first **L**, dropping down towards a farm. Turn **R** through a gate just before reaching the farm and follow the track into the woods.

**5** Keep following the track **SA** to a gate, after which the track becomes vague. Turn **L** and follow the wall to a gate in the diagonally opposite corner of the field.

**6** Go through the gate and turn **R** onto a good track. At the road, turn **L** (**SA** in effect) and follow the road downhill towards Castleton.

**Optional Route:** Take the first turning on the **R**. Follow this for 200m and turn **L** down a rocky track. Descend to the road and turn **L** to Castleton.

Once in Castleton, fork **L** at the green, and then keep **R** past the pub, heading roughly downhill until you reach the main road. It doesn't matter if you go the wrong way – you'll end up in the right place Turn **L** to return to the start.

## LocaL knowLeDge

The broken road up Mam Tor was the main route between Sheffield and Manchester, until it fell down the hill in the 1970s. When the road was built in 1802, the stability of the hillside was not thought to be a problem, as traffic was light and repairs could be easily made. As the volume of traffic increased and the tarmac weathered, the road began to crack and subside until, after a period of heavy rain, a landslide caused major damage and the road was closed.

## famILy RIDING

Castleton is a popular tourist spot that sees a lot of traffic on fine weekends, so it's not good for family riding. Head down to Ladybower Reservoir for a better option. Alternately, visit the castle or the showcaves in Castleton. Both are well worth visiting.

# HOUNDKIRK

route 16 // 14km

**A good introduction to the 'real' mountain biking the Peak District has to offer, but in a relatively small dose and without any big hills. You do, however, get a lot of rocks, some tricky little climbs and** (if you pick a wet day) **some massive puddles.**

The ride begins near the Fox House pub (a good spot for bar meals) before heading off towards Sheffield on Houndkirk Road – a wide track across Houndkirk and Burbage moors. This track is rocky, sandy and tricky in places, but at least you have the wind behind you – for now... The track undulates across the moor before dropping down to Ringinglow, climbing the road and then picking up another rocky bridleway heading back onto the moors. This track rattles and swoops its way back down to Houndkirk Road. You now retrace your steps (into the wind this time) to a fast descent to the road. You can now either return to your car or head off uphill for some more off-road, this time along grassy and muddy tracks. Watch out – in the summer, these are fast and fun, in the winter they are full of thigh-deep puddles and only fun if you like wet socks.

The Fox House pub, where this ride begins, lies on a very sharp bend in the A6187 above Hathersage, and is impossible to miss. There is a car park a short way along the road running away from the pub off the corner of the bend.

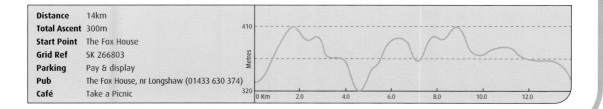

| | | |
|---|---|---|
| **Distance** | 14km | |
| **Total Ascent** | 300m | |
| **Start Point** | The Fox House | |
| **Grid Ref** | SK 266803 | |
| **Parking** | Pay & display | |
| **Pub** | The Fox House, nr Longshaw (01433 630 374) | |
| **Café** | Take a Picnic | |

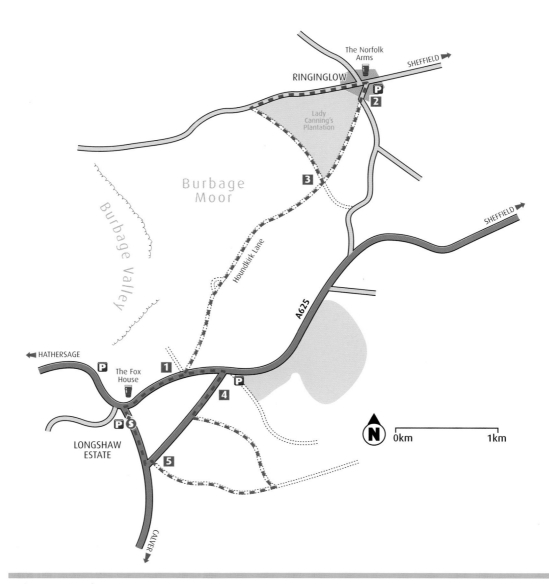

The Norfolk Arms

SHEFFIELD ▶

RINGINGLOW

Lady Canning's Plantation

**Burbage Moor**

**Burbage Valley**

3

Houndkirk Lane

SHEFFIELD ▶

A625

◀ HATHERSAGE

The Fox House

1

4

LONGSHAW ESTATE

5

CALVER

0km        1km

From the Fox House pub, follow the road uphill in the direction of Sheffield for 500m to a right hand bend.

**1** Turn **L** onto a stone-based track between two chevron signs, warning drivers of the bend. After 150m, continue **SA** through the gate directly ahead and start to climb.

At the top of the climb, follow the track around to the right and descend. Keep following this track as it undulates over varying terrain to a crossroads. Continue **SA** to a gate. Go through this and descend to the road.

**2** Turn **L** and ride to a T-junction in the centre of Ringinglow village. Turn **L** again and climb out of the village. **WARNING** – this road can be fast and busy.

Follow the road for just over 1km, until the plantation on your left gives way to open moorland. Turn **L** onto a signed bridleway through a gate and follow this alongside the plantation to a crossroads.

**3** Turn **R** and retrace your tyre tracks to the gate. Turn **L** immediately after the gate and follow the track to the road. Turn **L** again, climbing the road and turn **R** at the first junction.

**4** Climb the road (BUSY!) over the brow of the hill and turn **L** through a gate onto a signed bridleway. Follow this bridleway to a T-junction with a wider track – and usually a huge puddle. Turn sharp **R** and ride through the puddles to a gate.

**5** Turn **L** onto the road, **R** at the junction and follow the road down towards the Fox House and your car.

## Local knowledge
If you're trying to ride a narrow line between two large puddles (or rocks), don't focus on the thing you're trying to avoid. Look where you're going and the bike will (usually) go that way. Alternatively, you can buy waterproof socks from decent outdoor shops...

# Bakewell

route 17 // 12km

**Almost entirely off-road, this hilly loop around Bakewell and Chatsworth is a 'proper', albeit short, mountain bike ride. The terrain around Bakewell doesn't feature the large rocks and sand of the Dark Peak, with dirt and grass being the distinguishing trail characteristics of the ride. Whilst this makes for a ride that's never too technically demanding, it does mean that it can be very hard work in the wet.**

Starting from Bakewell, the ride heads out along the Monsal Trail and then follows the River Wye for a short distance before climbing on good tracks to the foot of the woods. Tricky climbing – there are a few slippery rocks to dodge and the odd steep section to grind up – leads to some swift descending through open fields and then a long, grassy swoop down to the road with great views out over Chatsworth House. The return climb begins in the old walled village of Edensor and then continues up a loose and gravelly slope, before turning off into the woods for a tricky descent into Bakewell.

This ride is equally good in either direction. The final descent into Bakewell (as described here) can be bypassed by sticking to the road to make an easier climb, or a fun road descent for those who don't fancy the woodland option.

To find the start, leave the centre of Bakewell, heading for Baslow and Sheffield. Immediately after crossing the bridge, turn **R** and follow the road uphill. Take the second left and then ride through the car park on your right to reach the Monsal Trail.

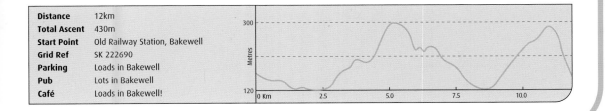

| Distance | 12km |
|---|---|
| Total Ascent | 430m |
| Start Point | Old Railway Station, Bakewell |
| Grid Ref | SK 222690 |
| Parking | Loads in Bakewell |
| Pub | Lots in Bakewell |
| Café | Loads in Bakewell! |

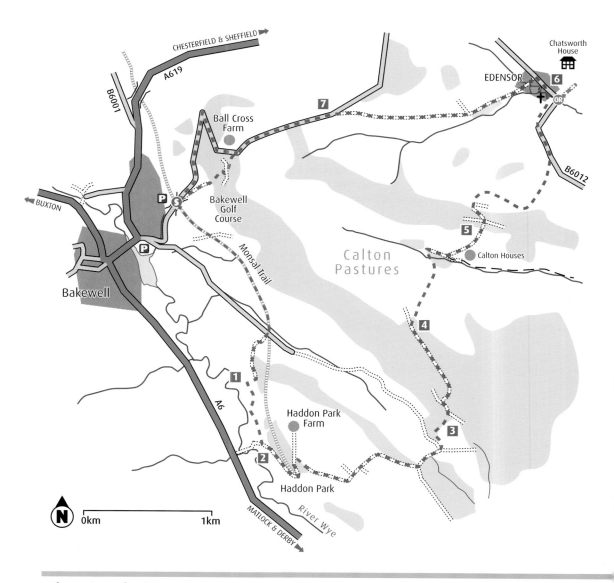

Turn **R** along the Monsal Trail, passing under a bridge almost immediately. Follow the trail until it ends and turn **R** off the trail and down the wide steps to the road.

Turn **L** and then almost immediately **R** onto a wide dirt track. Follow this track uphill and around to the left until a sign informs you that the road ahead is private. Turn **R** through a gate onto a bridleway running through a field.

**1** Ride **SA** into the field, keeping the fence on your right, heading towards the trees. Turn sharp **L** onto what appear to be sheep tracks and follow these parallel to the river to a gate. Go through the gate onto the tarmac lane and turn **L**.

**2** Follow the lane uphill around sharp bends until a signed bridleway runs through a gate on the **R** into a field. Follow the bridleway through the field to a good track. Follow this track for approximately 1km, to what appears to be a T-junction. Ignore the wide tracks to the left and right, and continue **SA** over the junction, through a narrow gap and onto a signed bridleway.

**3** Follow this bridleway uphill, climbing over some tricky ground to meet a wider track. Turn **L** and then, after only a few metres, turn **R** up a relatively wide track, climbing once again. The track soon levels off and twists and turns to a gate.

**4** Go through the gate and follow the track out into an open field. Whizz down to the woods ahead and through another gate. Turn **R** after the gate (don't go straight ahead) and then keep **L** where the bridleway splits. Follow the track as it climbs up into the field and into the woods once more.

**5** Go **SA** through the woods and more gates onto a grassy slope. Bears **R** passing well to the right of the clump of trees and ride down to the road. Turn **L**, and, as the road bends right, head **SA** across the grass – cutting the road corner and emerging right beside the walled village of Edensor.

**OPTIONAL ROUTE:** Well, not a route so much as a break! Turn **R**, and follow the lane down to the magnificent Chatsworth House. Lock your bikes and look round.

**6** Meeting the road, turn **L** almost immediately into the walled village. Follow the road to the **R** and continue **SA**, passing the church on your left. Climb the road and continue climbing as the road ends and the track begins. Don't be put off by the loose stone surface – things ease as you climb.

**7** Meeting the lane, continue **SA** up the hill. Just beyond the brow, immediately after a farm track on the left, turn **L** on a signed bridleway dropping steeply into the woods. **OR** for an easier descent continue **SA** down the road. This is a hard descent, full of roots and twists and turns. It's also great fun and emerges quickly in the middle of the golf course. DANGER – small white flying objects (eminently identifiable). Don't count on your helmet to save you!

Rejoin the road and cruise down over the bridge and turn **R** back towards the start of the ride.

## famiLy RIDING

Not really – this is off-road, going up and down a big hill. You could take the kids to Chatsworth House instead and while away the afternoon watching them pet the pigs and play in the adventure playground.

# beeley moor & darley dale

route 18 // 14.5km

A ride of two halves – off-road through the woods and up on the moors on quiet lanes. The ride begins high up above Darley Dale before dropping towards the village via a wide track. This track starts gently and makes for some fast riding, but becomes very rocky and technical for the last few hundred metres of its length. Luckily, this can be avoided by taking the parallel road if needed. Some road work leads along the hillside and to the first section of woodland – a short climb followed by a wooded traverse. The trail isn't hard, but is narrow in places. A quick road descent around hairpins leads to more woodland – a mixture of fast trails and easy climbing. Then it's a bit of a slog on grass and mud trails up to the road, which in turn climbs up onto the moors and back to the start.

To find the start, take the B5057 out of Darley Dale, heading for Chesterfield. As the road levels out and begins to run through woods, turn **L** at a crossroads onto a narrow lane. The ride starts at the obvious sharp bend 1.5km along this lane.

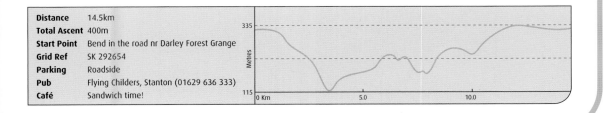

| | |
|---|---|
| **Distance** | 14.5km |
| **Total Ascent** | 400m |
| **Start Point** | Bend in the road nr Darley Forest Grange |
| **Grid Ref** | SK 292654 |
| **Parking** | Roadside |
| **Pub** | Flying Childers, Stanton (01629 636 333) |
| **Café** | Sandwich time! |

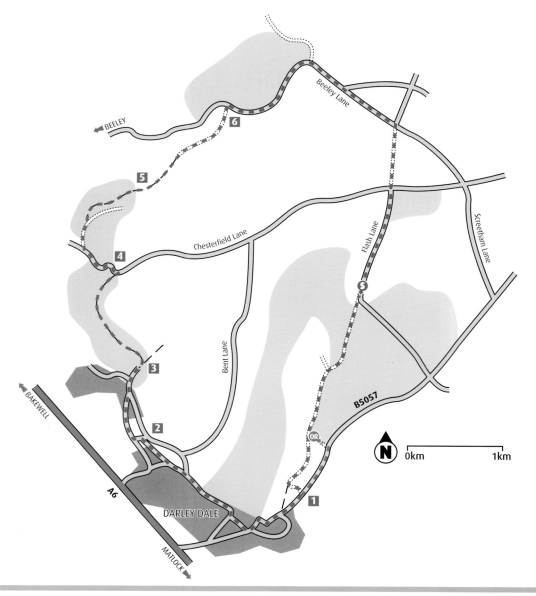

BEELEY

Beeley Lane

6

5

4

Chesterfield Lane

Flash Lane

Screetham Lane

S

Bent Lane

3

2

BAKEWELL

A6

DARLEY DALE

B5057

OR

1

N

0km          1km

MATLOCK

From your car, find your way to the sharp bend in the road and take the wide dirt track heading off downhill from the outside of the bend. Descend, ignoring turnings until you reach tarmac near Woodside Farm. As the tarmac bends sharply to the left, assess the rocky track continuing **SA** and then:

**A)** rattle down it over the rocks to the road, or

**B)** follow the tarmac lane to the left and then turn **R** at the main road.

**1** Follow the road downhill around some sharp bends and then take the first **R** onto a narrow lane. Follow this lane between houses to a T-junction and turn **R**, climbing relatively and ignoring turnings to the left and right as the gradient eases and the road descends to a second T-junction.

**2** Turn **L**, and then **R** at the next T-junction. Climb gently uphill, taking the second **R** up Lumb Lane (with a dead-end road sign), shortly before the road starts to descend. Follow this lane until it levels out, bear **R** onto grass and head into the woods.

**3** Climb about 100m and then turn **L** onto a narrow bridleway near the top of the woods. Follow this undulating trail through the woods to reach several gates. Continue **SA** through these gates and follow the bridleway through the woods until you arrive at the road. Turn **L** and descend steeply around hairpins for about 250m.

**4** Just after a house on the right, turn **R** onto a wide dirt track signed Haddon Estate. Climb gently for 200m before turning **L** onto a signed bridleway dropping into the woods. Follow this good track downhill and then keep on it as it begins to climb to a wooden bridge. Cross this bridge and then turn sharp **R** and climb to a gate.

**5** Go through this gate and climb into fields. Keep climbing on grass to a wide dirt track by a barn and turn **L** onto this. Go through the gate and follow the track **SA** as it climbs through fields of cows and then descends to a road.

**6** Turn **R** and, with the woods to your right and a big bank of bright green bracken to your left, climb up the road onto the moor. Turn **R** onto a wide dirt track (opposite the second lane on your left). Follow this to the road and continue **SA** down the lane opposite to your car.

# family RIDING

The majority of routes in this book are not suitable for young children – they are either too tiring, too tricky or too demanding (the rides, not the children...). Several of the rides do begin near more suitable riding, and we've indicated this where it's applicable. However, to save you the trouble of searching through the routes, here are some suggestions for where to take children/complete beginners out for a gentle ride.

NOTE: The Peak District has several old railway lines which have been converted into good, wide tracks. Well surfaced and away from the traffic, they are ideal for riding with children of any age. We've given these tracks their own section – see page 99 for detailed information.

# Ladybower & Derwent Reservoirs

| | |
|---|---|
| **Distance:** | Anything up to 20km |
| **Map:** | OS Explorer OL 1 Dark Peak |
| **Starting points:** | Fairholmes, Ladybower Bridge |
| **Grid Ref:** | SK 172893, SK 203858 |
| **Parking:** | Lots of car parks in the area |
| **Cycle Hire:** | Derwent Cycle Hire, Fairholmes: 01433 651 261 |
| **Visitor Centres:** | Fairholmes |
| **Facilities:** | Café, bike hire, toilets |

**Ladybower reservoir straddles the A57 in the centre of the Dark Peak, at the junction with the A6013.**

The easily accessed reservoirs in the heart of the Dark Peak are massively popular with cyclists, and for good reason. The car park at Fairholmes, sandwiched between the reservoirs, boasts bike hire, toilets and a café (complete with ducks to feed/ keep your rolls away from) and is possibly the most popular starting point in the Peak. Wide, smooth and predominantly traffic-free trails head north up both sides of the reservoirs in an exceptionally pretty part of the national park. Either ride for as long as you feel is appropriate before turning back, or see page 17 for a complete loop around the reservoirs.

# carsington water

| | |
|---|---|
| **Distance:** | A 13km circuit of the reservoir |
| **Map:** | OS Explorer OL 24 White Peak |
| **Starting points:** | Carsington Water Visitor Centre |
| **Grid Ref:** | SK 241517 |
| **Parking:** | Pay & display |
| **Cycle Hire:** | Carsington Sports and Leisure: 01629 540 478 |
| **Visitor Centres:** | Carsington Water: 01629 540 478 www.carsingtonwater.com |
| **Facilities:** | Cafés, toilets, bike hire, gift shop... and more! |

**Carsington Water is well signposted and lies between Ashbourne and Wirksworth, just outside the southern boundary of the Peak District National Park.**

A popular eight-mile cycle route runs around Carsington Water, Britain's ninth largest reservoir. Starting from the visitor centre, the relatively hilly route circles the reservoir, passing through carefully managed woodland and the stone village of Hopton, where you can take a breather at the local pub. The trail is predominantly on a good concrete surface, although it does cross some busy roads.

The site was awarded a "Forestry Centre of Excellence" for its management of the local woodland, which is home to a wide variety of wildlife, most notably the birds who reside at the lake. You can watch them from two purpose-built hides and from the conservation area on the far side of the lake.

Back at the visitor centre, there's a large adventure playground, a designated barbeque area and opportunities to go horse riding, sailing or canoeing. The centre itself houses a permanent exhibition explaining the role of water in our lives, a café and souvenir shop.

Don't leave without a look at the Kugel Stone in the centre of the courtyard. This ball of granite weighs over a tonne and sits on a thin layer of water under pressure, allowing you to move it with the touch (well, a shove) of your hand.

LINACRE RESERVOIRS

SEVERN TRENT WATER

# Linacre reservoirs

| | |
|---|---|
| **Distance:** | About 3.5km around the reservoirs, with various options |
| **Map:** | OS Explorer OL 24 White Peak |
| **Starting points:** | Linacre Woods Car Parks |
| **Grid Ref:** | SK 336727 |
| **Parking:** | Free parking, Linacre Woods car parks |
| **Cycle Hire:** | None |
| **Visitor Centres:** | There are various information boards in the woods |
| **Facilities:** | Toilets, ice cream van in the summer |

**Linacre Woods is signposted off the B6050, between Cutthorpe and Prathall.**

Situated right on the edge of Chesterfield, the three Linacre reservoirs have some well-surfaced and wide trails running around them. The carved wooden maps on site show where you can and can't ride. On the subject of wood carvings, look out for the various totem poles, sculptures and carvings on the way round (often in the trees themselves). Some sections can become a little muddy in the winter, but you can ride here year-round without getting too bogged down.

# railway trails

During the eighteenth century, several railway lines were constructed to serve the towns and villages of the Peak District. Several of these lines eventually closed, and, once the tracks had been taken up, many were re-opened as some of the first recreational trails in the country. Handily, Steam engines, despite their mechanical innards, view steep climbs in a similar way to many cyclists – as obstacles to be avoided – and so these trails are generally relatively flat, wide and well-surfaced trails. Perfect!

# HIGH peak trail

| | |
|---|---|
| **Distance:** | Up to 27km each way along a disused railway line |
| **Map:** | OS Landranger 119 Buxton and Matlock |
| **Starting points:** | This trail can be started from the north at Parsley Hay, the High Peak Junction at the south or Middleton Top visitor centre, about two thirds of the way down the trail |
| **Grid Ref:** | SK 276552 – SK 110673 |
| **Parking:** | There is a pay and display car park at Parsley Hay, and parking is also available at Middleton Top and High Peak Junction |
| **Cycle Hire:** | Middleton Top: 01629 823 204<br>Parsley Hay: 01298 84493 |
| **Visitor Centres:** | Middleton Top: 01629 823 204<br>Parsley Hay: 01298 84493 |

A well-known and popular route, the High Peak Trail follows the course of the old Cromford and High Peak Railway which, completed in 1830, was among the earliest in the country. It runs from Parsley Hay at its north end down to Cromford Canal in the south, and is probably most easily ridden as a 'there-and-back' route. It's worth pointing out that the trail does literally run down from north to south, with the steepest sections at the southern end and you should bear this in mind when deciding how far along the route you wish to ride. Unlike many railway routes, the High Peak Trail twists and turns surprisingly sharply as it runs through the limestone scenery of the White Peak, so the view changes regularly. Back at Parsley Hay, the trail meets the Tissington Trail, so you can always head off down this if you're still feeling lively.

Middleton Top, about two thirds of the way down the trail, sits at the top of the Middleton incline and houses a steam winding engine, built in 1892 to haul wagons up and down the incline. It can be seen running on the first weekend of each month in the summer, and on bank holidays. Further south, near High Peak Junction, is the Cromford Canal, where several remnants of the area's historical importance as an industrial centre are still maintained as part of the Derwent Valley Mills World Heritage Site.

# monsal trail

| | |
|---|---|
| **Distance:** | 15km each way along a spectacular disused railway line |
| **Map:** | the trail is well signposted, and a leaflet with map is available from the National Park website: www.peakdistrict.gov.uk |
| **Starting points:** | Bakewell, Hassop, Millers Dale Stations |
| **Grid Ref:** | SK 230679; SK 217705; SK 104725 |
| **Parking:** | Pay & display at various stations on route |
| **Cycle Hire:** | Bakewell Bikes: 01629 815 077 |
| | Hassop Station Cycle Hire: 01629 810 588 |
| | Blackwell Mill Cycle Hire: 01298 708 38 |
| **Visitor Centres:** | Information points on route and in National Park Visitor Centre in Bakewell: 01629 816 558 |

**Following the old Midland Railway through the centre of the Peak, the Monsal Trail is one of the finest easy rides in northern England. Starting at Blackwell Mill near Buxton, it runs south for 15 kilometres, passing through (literally!) some of the Peak's most spectacular limestone countryside via a series of tunnels, cuttings and embankments.**

Information points along the way highlight the remarkable feats of engineering involved in the construction of the line, while, in beautiful contrast, eleven nature reserves lie within a mile of the trail. Although some of their more secretive inhabitants – like otters – aren't easily seen, dippers, buzzards, hares and the odd fox are everyday sights along the route.

The full route has only recently (2011) opened to the public. Previously, a shortened version ran across the fields from Bakewell to Little Longstone, where the rail line disappeared into the Headstone Tunnel beneath Monsal Head. This, and the following three tunnels were closed for safety reasons and while walkers could bypass them, cyclists were stuck. Now, the tunnels have been renovated, lit (during daylight hours) and opened, adding a touch of excitement to the route and allowing access to the spectacular northern end of the trail as it carves through the rugged limestone gorge of Chee Dale.

Access is easy at Hassop, Bakewell and Millers Dale stations. Cyclists can also join the trail at Coombs Viaduct, near Bakewell. Walkers and cyclists are advised to park at the Bakewell Agricultural Centre and access Coombs Road via the footpath at the back of the centre.

# manifold way

| | |
|---|---|
| **Distance:** | Up to 14km each way |
| **Map:** | OS Explorer OL 24 White Peak |
| **Starting points:** | Hulme End, Waterhouses, or any of the car parks along the length of the trail |
| **Grid Ref:** | SK 105596 – SK 091501 |
| **Parking:** | Pay & display at Hulme End<br>several along the length of the trail |
| **Cycle Hire:** | Manifold Valley Bikes: 01538 308 609<br>Brown End Farm: 01538 308 313<br>(both in Waterhouses) |
| **Visitor Centres:** | Hulme End |

**The Manifold Way sits right at the bottom of the Peak District, following the line of the former Leek and Manifold Light Railway. Opened in 1937, three years after the railway closed, the trail is almost completely flat and well surfaced throughout the whole of its 14km length. Unlike the other trails, a short section of the Manifold Way is shared with traffic, but don't let this put you off, as the rest of the trail is very easy cycling.**

The Manifold Way runs through the attractive valleys created by the Manifold and Hamps rivers. Much of the area is designated a Site of Special Scientific Interest, due to the various plants and the geology of the area. Look out for the massive and impressive (massively impressive?) Thor's Cave near Wetton. You might also be lucky enough to spot deer, foxes, badgers or weasels in the woods around the trail, although it's probably best to avoid busy Sundays if you have this in mind.

There are car parks at various points along the length of the trail, and cafés at Wetton Mill and Lee House.

# tissington trail

| | |
|---|---|
| **Distance:** | Up to 21km each way along a disused railway |
| **Map:** | OS Landranger 119 Buxton and Matlock |
| **Starting points:** | Ashbourne Cycle Hire, Parsley Hay |
| **Grid Ref:** | SK 147637 – SK 175472 |
| **Parking:** | Pay & display, Parsley Hay |
| **Cycle Hire:** | Ashbourne Cycle Hire: 01335 343 156 Parsley Hay: 01298 84493 |
| **Visitor Centres:** | Ashbourne: 01335 343 666 Parsley Hay: 01298 84493 |

**The Tissington Trail is another well-known route that follows the tracks of a disused railway line. As with the High Peak Trail, there is a gentle drop as the trail runs south – nothing too severe but a possible consideration when planning a ride. Get the climbing out of the way when you've plenty of energy on the way out and you'll have forgotten all about it by the time you've blasted easily back to the car! This time, the former railway was the Ashbourne to Buxton line, completed in 1899 and closed in 1967. Four years later it then became one of the first lines to be re-opened as a recreational trail.**

The Tissington Trail meets the High Peak Trail just south of Parsley Hay, so there's nothing stopping you linking them. A technically easy but long ride would be a big loop from Ashbourne: climb the Tissington Trail to Parsley Hay and then drop down the High Peak trail to the B5056, which leads back into Ashbourne.

# Longdendale trail

**Distance:**       19km (Glossop to Woodhead)
                    9km (Woodhead to Penistone)

**Map:**            OS Explorer OL 1 Dark Peak

**Starting points:** Hadfield, Torside, Crowden,
                     Dunford Bridge, Penistone

**Grid Ref:**       SK 025963 – SK 113998 and
                    SK 163029 – SK 245034

**Parking:**        Hadfield, Torside, Crowden,
                    Dunford Bridge, Penistone

**Cycle Hire:**     None

**Visitor Centres:** Torside

**The Longdendale Trail forms part of the Trans Pennine Trail, which runs from coast to coast across the country. We've included the section of the TPT which runs from Woodhead to Penistone under this listing as, like the Longdendale Trail, it runs along the course of the old Sheffield – Manchester railway line.**

The Longdendale Trail runs along the course of the former Woodhead Railway and now forms part of the Trans Pennine Trail. It traverses the top of the Peak from Glossop to Penistone, roughly along the same line as the Woodhead Pass, or A628. The trail is split into two halves by the Woodhead Tunnel, which is now closed, with one half running for around 19km from Hadfield, near Glossop, to the tunnel, and the second half leaving Winscar Reservoir, at the other end of the tunnel, for Penistone.

As with the other tails, there are several car parks and visitor centres along the length of the trail, all of which would make nice starting points for a ride, and several information boards along the way.

Personally, we'd recommend riding the Glossop half of the trail as the surroundings are slightly nicer. The trail runs uphill away from Hadfield, so starting here means that you get all the climbing out of the way early on, and an easy cruise back once you've turned around.

# sett valley trail

| | |
|---|---|
| **Distance:** | Up to 4km each way |
| **Map:** | OS Explorer OL 1 Dark Peak |
| **Starting points:** | Hayfield or New Mills (the trail is signed at both ends) |
| **Grid Ref:** | SK 036869 – SK 001855 |
| **Parking:** | Dedicated pay & display in Hayfield |
| **Cycle Hire:** | None |
| **Visitor Centres:** | Hayfield Countryside Centre: 01663 746 222 |

The Sett Valley Trail is a little shorter than other Peak cycleways. Linking Hayfield and New Mills, it is only 4km long and runs parallel to the River Sett. The surface is good and the riding easy. The trail does rise slightly as it runs towards Hayfield, but the facilities are better in Hayfield so start there, cruise down to the impressive viaducts of New Mills, turn round and head back to the Royal for Sunday lunch.

# appendix

## visitor centres

Shared website: **www.peakdistrict.gov.uk**

**Bakewell** 01629 816 558
bakewell@peakdistrict.gov.uk

**Castleton** 01433 816 572
castleton@peakdistrict.gov.uk

**Edale** 01433 670 207
edale@peakdistrict.gov.uk

**Fairholmes** 01433 650 953
(Upper Derwent) derwentinfo@hotmail.co.uk

## maps

OS Explorer OL1: The Peak District – Dark Peak Area, 1:25,000

OS Explorer OL24: The Peak District – White Peak Area, 1:25,000

Central Peak District, AA Leisure Map, 1:50,000

## bike shops

**18 Bikes** off the main road in Hope
01433 621 111
www.18bikes.co.uk

**Bike Garage** High Peak Garden Centre, Hope Valley
01433 659 345
www.bikegarage.co.uk

**The Bike Factory** Beech Road, Whaley Bridge
01663 735 020
www.ukbikefactory.com

**High Peak Cycles** Glossop
01457 861 535
www.highpeakcycles.co.uk

**Mark Anthony** Spring Gardens, Buxton
01298 220 02
www.activesport.co.uk

**Sett Valley Cycles** Union Road, New Mills
01633 742 629
www.settvalleycycles.co.uk

**Stanley Fearns** Bakewell Road, Matlock
01629 582 089
www.stanleyfearns.co.uk

## Bike Hire

| | |
|---|---|
| **Bike Garage** | High Peak Garden Centre, Hope Valley, 01433 659 345 www.bikegarage.co.uk |
| **Derwent Cycle Hire** | Fairholmes, Upper Derwent 01433 651 261 |
| **Bakewell Bikes** | off Coombs Road, Bakewell 01629 815 077 www.bakewellbikes.co.uk |
| **Alive Bike Hire** | Castleton Road, Hope 07538 892 065 www.alivebikehire.co.uk |
| **Carsington Sports and Leisure** | Carsington Water 01629 540 478 www.carsingtonwater.com |
| **Middleton Top Cycle Hire** | nr Middleton by Wirksworth 01629 823 204 www.visitpeakdistrict.com |
| **Hassop Station** | on the B6001 near Bakewell 01629 810 588 www.hassopstation.co.uk |
| **Parsley Hay Cycle Hire** | nr Buxton 01298 844 93 www.peakdistrict.gov.uk |
| **Blackwell Mill Cycle Hire** | off the A6 nr Topley Pike, 01298 708 38 www.peakblackwellcyclehire.com |

## Accommodation

You're spoilt for choice when looking for somewhere to stay in the Peak. Not only is there accommodation everywhere, but there are at least two comprehensive sites for finding it: **www.peakdistrictonline.co.uk** and **www.visitpeakdistrict.com**

### Camping

There are campsites all over the place. If you want something basic, try North Lees (01433 650 838) under Stanage Edge. For something central in the Dark Peak, head for Edale – Fieldhead (01433 670 386, **www.fieldhead-campsite.co.uk**) and Upper Booth Farm (01433 670 250, **www.upperbooth camping.co.uk**). Further south, near Bakewell, try Lathkill Dale (01629 813 521, **www.lathkilldalecampsite.co.uk**), Greenhills Holiday Park (01629 813 052, **www.greenhills holidaypark.co.uk**) or Park House Campsite near Monsal Head, 01629 640 463.

There are Youth Hostels throughout the Hope Valley in the Dark Peak (Castleton, Hathersage, Edale) and several in the White Peak, (Eyam, Bakewell, Bretton, Youlgreave and Matlock). Visit: **www.yha.org.uk**

## cafés

The Peak District is fully geared up for mid and post-ride refuelling sessions. Cafes vary from the most twee of the twee to the greasiest spoon. Here's a selection – near the rides – that are recommended by the team:

| | |
|---|---|
| **Bakewell** | So full of cafés that we couldn't recommend one over the others! |
| **Outside Café** | Baslow Road, Calver<br>01433 631 111 |
| **The Eating House** | Calver Bridge, Calver<br>01433 631 583 |
| **Penny Pot Cafe** | nr the Station, Edale<br>01433 670 293 |
| **Eyam Tea Rooms** | The Square, Eyam<br>01433 631 274 |
| **Outside Cafe** | Main Road, Hathersage<br>01433 651 936 |
| **Poolside Café** | Oddfellows Road, Hathersage<br>01433 650 843 |
| **Hassop Station** | on the B6001 near Bakewell<br>01629 815 668 |
| **Woodbine Café** | Castleton Road, Hope<br>07778 113 882 |
| **Roaches Tea Rooms** | Roach Road<br>01538 300 345 |
| **Caudwell's Mill** | Rowsley<br>01629 733 185 |

## PUBS

There are lots of good pubs in the Peak District – all well worth visiting for post or mid-ride refreshment. Here's a selection close to the routes in this guide.

| | |
|---|---|
| **The Old Nag's Head** | Edale<br>01433 670 291<br>www.the-old-nags-head.co.uk |
| **The Cheshire Cheese Inn** | Hope<br>01433 620 381<br>www.thecheshirecheeseinn.co.uk<br>(accommodation) |
| **The Yorkshire Bridge** | Ladybower Reservoir<br>01433 651 361<br>www.yorkshire-bridge.co.uk<br>(accommodation) |
| **The Barrel Inn** | Bretton<br>01433 630 856<br>www.thebarrelinn.co.uk<br>(accommodation) |
| **The Crispin Inn** | Great Longstone<br>01629 640 237<br>www.thecrispingreatlongstone.co.uk |
| **Monsal Head Hotel** | Monsal Head<br>01629 640 250<br>www.monsalhead.com<br>(amazing location, accommodation) |

## other publications/websites

**Peak District Mountain Biking – Dark Peak Trails**
Jon Barton, Vertebrate Publishing

**White Peak Mountain Biking – The Pure Trails**
Jon Barton, Vertebrate Publishing

**Day Walks in the Peak District – 20 classic circular routes**
Norman Taylor & Barry Pope, Vertebrate Publishing

**Day Walks in the Peak District – 20 new circular routes**
Norman Taylor & Barry Pope, Vertebrate Publishing

## about the authors

**Tom Fenton**
Tom edits and writes guidebooks for Vertebrate Publishing, spending half his time checking for missing commas and the other half out riding his bike, 'researching routes for work'.

**Jon Barton**
Jon is a veteran writer of bestselling Peak District guidebooks. Having lived in the heart of the Peak, he certainly knows his subject and his guides have been read by thousands. Of course, cycling around the Peak for a living isn't the perfect job it sounds – all those summer evenings riding bikes, testing pubs, comparing one café with another...

## about the photographer

**John Houlihan** at **Witness Photography**
John is an enthusiastic cyclist, veteran of many mountain biking competitions and winner of a few, he is as happy leading the race as he is towing his young son. A full time photojournalist, his work is regularly commissioned by the Sunday Times, The Guardian and What Mountain Bike among many. He is currently chairman of the Trail Cyclist Association, the national governing body for MTBO in the UK.

## vertebrate publishing

Vertebrate Publishing designs, produces and publishes bestselling outdoor books and guides. Titles include the company's own **Dark Peak Mountain Biking** – True Grit Trails, the MLTUK's **Hill Walking** – The Official Handbook of the Mountain Leader and Walking Group Leader Schemes, which is a bestselling outdoor title for three years running and the FRCC's award-winning **Lake District Rock** – Selected Rock Climbs in the Lake District.

For more information please visit our website:
**www.v-publishing.co.uk** or email **info@v-publishing.co.uk**

# Hassop STATION
## CAFE

&

# Monsal TRAIL
## CYCLE HIRE

Cafe, cycle hire, bookshop & gifts on the scenic Monsal Trail, 1 mile north of Bakewell.

Open 9am-5pm, seven days a week

One mile north of Bakewell on the A6020 / B6001 roundabout

DE45 1NW

TO SHEFFIELD & CHESTERFIELD

WE ARE HERE

A6020

TO BUXTON
A6

ASHFORD IN THE WATER

B6001

A619

Monsal Trail

A6

BAKEWELL

A6

TO MATLOCK